CALICO **Cooks!**

RECIPES AND DECORATING TIPS FROM

CALICO CORNERS®

PICTURED CLOCKWISE ARE:
Pear Tart, page 181
Lemon Soufflé, page 148
Berry Cloud with Brandied Cream, page 139
Apples in Baskets, page 149

CALICO Cooks!

RECIPES AND DECORATING TIPS FROM

CALICO CORNERS®

CALICO **Cooks!**

Published by Calico Corners
Copyright © 1999 by Calico Corners,
   a division of Everfast, Inc.
203 Gale Lane, Kennett Square, Pennsylvania 19348
1-800-213-6366

Executive Editor: Jan Jessup
Project Assistant: Margaret Jendrejzak

*All of the profits from the sale of this cookbook will be donated
to support breast cancer research.*

Edited, designed, and manufactured in the
   United States of America by
Favorite Recipes® Press, an imprint of

FRP™

2451 Atrium Way
Nashville, Tennessee 37214

Book Design: Bruce Gore
Managing Editor: Mary Cummings
Project Manager: Jane Hinshaw
Production Manager: Mark Sloan
Project Production: Sara Anglin

Library of Congress Number: 99-094627
ISBN: 0-9669445-0-X
First Printing: 1999 12,500 copies

DEDICATION

Calico Cooks! is dedicated to all those in our company and among our customers whose lives have been affected by breast cancer. Unfortunately, that's getting to be more and more of us, female and male.

Perhaps because her loss is so recent, we especially wish to honor the memory of Jill Sewell, who managed the Calico Corners store in Pasadena, California, for nine years. Jill died in 1998 at age 46 of breast cancer, knowing that this book was under way. When Jill's cancer was diagnosed the previous year, she was in the midst of buying her first house. Not knowing what the future would bring, she wondered if she should go through with the purchase. Jill shared those worries with a counselor at the Susan G. Komen Foundation in Dallas, Texas. The counselor responded with two pointed questions. "Well, Jill, are you planning to live? Or are you planning to die?"

Jill immediately decided to buy the house. She loved being there. And she was extraordinarily courageous in fighting her disease, even getting into a lottery for an experimental treatment. Jill's life and untimely death strengthens our commitment to support research into prevention and treatment of breast cancer, which touches the lives of so many co-workers, mothers, sisters, daughters, and friends.

CONTENTS

Preface   6

Introduction   7

Brunch • Breads   8

Appetizers • Beverages   30

Soups • Salads   46

Meats • Poultry • Seafood   68

Vegetables • Side Dishes   98

Pasta   118

Desserts • Candy • Cookies   138

Cakes • Pies   162

Contributor List   184

Fabric Notes   186

Index   187

Order Information   192

PREFACE

This cookbook is a labor of love and hope from hundreds of store managers, sales associates, district managers, and corporate employees in more than 110 Calico Corners stores across the United States. There are three great loves that seem to drive the members of the Calico family: first, a passion for fabrics and decorating; second, an overwhelming desire to help customers create beautiful homes and have fun in the process; and finally, a great love of good food and good times.

The elements of design that go into creating a lovely room are similar to the principles that are used by great cooks. Color, texture, composition, balance, and proportion are as critical to an appealing plate of food as they are to a pleasing room. There is a creative aspect to both cooking and decorating, a desire to nurture friends and family and self.

Within each Calico Corners store, there are numerous occasions that are marked with a party, a birthday cake, a celebratory dinner or potluck supper. And fortunately many of the talented people who have such a love of fabrics also share a passion for cooking. The pages of their recipe books are stained, annotated, dog-eared, and bookmarked. Recipes are traded joyfully with family and friends. Cooking magazines are saved for just one favorite recipe. And cookbooks can be read as though they were racy novels. When this project was announced, over 500 favorite recipes were contributed from Calico Corners stores all across the country. We wish we could have published them all.

We also extend special thanks to our employees who first suggested publishing a cookbook to raise additional funds for breast cancer research. One of the most involved was Margaret Jendrejzak, an in-home consultant at Calico Corners in Williamsville (Buffalo), New York. Margaret worked with us and the editors at FRP to shape, edit, and promote this book. We particularly appreciate the enthusiastic support of FRP Managing Editor Mary Cummings and Project Manager Jane Hinshaw, who shared our belief in this book and this cause. We hope you enjoy this book as much as we enjoyed developing it. Happy cooking!

Jan Jessup
Executive Editor

Stuart Brown
Vice President

INTRODUCTION

What makes Calico Corners legendary?

Enthusiasm, incredible values, and outstanding service. We think it's a combination of all three. At Calico Corners, you can have fun decorating exactly the way you want. Coordinating two fabrics for a reversible duvet? That's easy! In search of a new sofa now that the kids are grown? We can help! When it comes to home fashions, if you can dream it, we can help you make it a reality.

Passion for fabrics. We love helping home decorators discover their own unique style as they create interiors that feel like home. And with thousands of fabrics and custom trims to choose from, you'll have plenty of creative options at your fingertips. Our experienced staff can answer your decorating questions while providing ideas and imagination.

Custom furniture built for you. Pick your frame, then pick your fabrics. That's how Calico Corners makes custom furniture affordable. With all the fabric choices in our stores, plus those shown in our catalog, the only difficult part will be trying to decide which fabric is your favorite.

Custom workrooms for effortless decorating. Our stores will gladly custom-make anything you desire—decorative pillows, window treatments, duvets and bed dressings, tableskirts, even reupholstery. We'll help you detail your project any way you wish. Tailored pleats? Of course! Contrast welting? Absolutely! Ruffles and bows? Why not? Bring us your ideas and we'll take care of everything from fabrication to installation.

Superb values. The only thing better than finding fabrics you love is finding them at terrific savings. Whether choosing first-quality fabrics—including many exclusive to Calico Corners—or our carefully selected seconds, you'll be delighted by how affordable they all are.

Current catalogs. Dial 1-800-213-6366 for a free issue of our current catalog. It's brimming with great fabrics and inspiring decorating ideas.

Fabrics, furniture and inspiration.

BRUNCH · BREADS

FALL MIMOSAS

raspberry-cranberry juice

Champagne

A festive touch to fall and winter entertaining or to celebrate the holidays. The recipe can also be varied to suit the season.

1 Mix an equal amount of the raspberry-cranberry juice and Champagne and pour over ice in a glass for each serving.

2 For Spring Mimosas, substitute orange juice for the raspberry-cranberry juice and add about 1 teaspoon of Triple Sec or Cointreau to each glass.

MAKES A VARIABLE AMOUNT

BANANA CITRUS COMPOTE

¾ **cup water**

¾ **cup sugar**

2 **tablespoons julienned lime zest**

1 **tablespoon julienned lemon zest**

1 **tablespoon julienned orange zest**

8 **ripe bananas**

juice of 1 lime

Served in clear glass bowls, this can be either the perfect ending or beginning for a winter brunch.

1 Combine the water and sugar in a small heavy saucepan and mix well. Bring to a boil. Stir in the lime zest, lemon zest and orange zest. Boil for 3 minutes, stirring occasionally. Remove from the heat and let stand for 10 minutes.

2 Cut the bananas diagonally into ½-inch slices. Toss with the lime juice in a bowl. Pour the warm syrup over the bananas, stirring to coat. Let stand at room temperature for just 30 minutes; do not let the bananas marinate too long as they become mushy.

3 Spoon into glass dessert bowls or goblets and serve immediately.

SERVES 6 TO 8

SLICED ORANGES WITH BERRY COULIS

1 (12-ounce) package fresh
   cranberries

1¼ cups sugar

1 cup fresh orange juice

3 or 4 (8-ounce) packages fresh
   raspberries

½ cup water
   grated zest of 1 orange

⅓ cup Triple Sec or Cointreau

6 oranges, peeled, cut into ½-inch
   slices
   sprigs of mint (optional)

This is festive enough for Christmas morning, and you can make the coulis a day or two in advance.

1 Combine the cranberries, sugar and orange juice in a saucepan and mix well. Simmer for 15 minutes, stirring occasionally. Stir in the raspberries, water and orange zest.

2 Simmer for 15 minutes, stirring occasionally. Strain the cranberry mixture through a fine sieve into a bowl. Stir in the Triple Sec. Cool to room temperature.

3 Spoon a small amount of the berry coulis into the center of each of 6 dessert plates. Fan the slices of 1 orange over each puddle. Drizzle with additional berry coulis and top with mint.

SERVES 6

BROCCOLI EGG BAKE

1 loaf firm white bread, crusts
   trimmed, cubed

3 cups milk

2 cups chopped ham

2 cups shredded Cheddar cheese

2 cups cooked chopped broccoli

7 jumbo eggs, beaten

½ teaspoon dry mustard

2 cups crushed cornflakes

1 cup shredded Cheddar cheese

⅓ cup melted butter

1 Mix the bread cubes, milk, ham, 2 cups cheese, broccoli, eggs and dry mustard in a bowl. Spoon into a 9x13-inch baking dish. Chill, covered, for 8 to 10 hours.

2 Mix the cornflakes, 1 cup cheese and butter in a bowl. Sprinkle over the egg mixture. Bake at 350 degrees for 1 hour.

SERVES 8 TO 10

BEEFY EGG BRUNCH

4   slices bacon, chopped

8   ounces dried beef or chopped ham

1   or 2 cans sliced mushrooms, drained

¼   cup butter

½   cup flour

4   cups milk

       pepper to taste

16   eggs

1   cup evaporated milk

¼   teaspoon salt

¼   cup butter, softened

Add a small amount of white wine with the milk for a richer flavor.

1   Fry the bacon in a skillet just until crisp. Add the dried beef, mushrooms and ¼ cup butter and mix well. Stir in the flour and cook until bubbly. Stir in the milk and pepper. Cook until thickened, stirring constantly.

2   Whisk the eggs, evaporated milk and salt in a bowl. Scramble the egg mixture in ¼ cup butter in a skillet.

3   Spoon a small amount of the mushroom mixture into a buttered baking dish. Layer the eggs and remaining mushroom mixture ½ at a time in the prepared dish. Sprinkle with additional mushrooms if desired. Bake, covered, at 275 degrees for up to 1 hour or until heated through.

4   This may be prepared 1 day in advance and stored, covered, in the refrigerator. Bake just before serving.

SERVES 12

Make a lighter, brighter coverlet for your bed in spring. Store the bedspread and stash the down duvet. Layer on a light coverlet made from a matelassé, a washed damask, or a textured solid. Add banding, a monogram, or a ruffle to make it unique.

Mexican Egg Puff

10 eggs

2 cups cottage cheese

8 ounces Swiss cheese, shredded

8 ounces Monterey Jack cheese, shredded

½ cup melted butter

1 (4-ounce) can chopped green chiles, drained

½ cup flour

1 teaspoon baking powder

½ teaspoon salt

Serve with salsa or taco sauce and crushed corn chips, and don't forget the corn bread on the side.

1 Beat the eggs in a bowl. Stir in the cottage cheese, Swiss cheese, Monterey Jack cheese, butter and chiles. Mix the flour, baking powder and salt in a bowl. Add to the egg mixture and mix well.

2 Spoon into a greased 9x13-inch baking pan. Bake at 350 degrees for 35 minutes.

SERVES 8

Mushroom Spinach Strata

8 slices firm white bread, crusts removed

1 pound fresh mushrooms, sliced

1 cup chopped onion

2 tablespoons butter or margarine

1 cup shredded Swiss cheese

1 (10-ounce) package frozen chopped spinach, thawed, drained

2 cups milk

3 eggs

1 teaspoon salt

¼ teaspoon nutmeg

⅛ teaspoon pepper

1 Cut the bread slices diagonally into halves. Arrange 6 halves over the bottom of a greased 10-inch pie plate. Sauté the mushrooms and onion in the butter in a skillet until tender; drain.

2 Layer ¾ of the mushroom mixture, cheese and spinach in the prepared pie plate; reserve the remaining mushroom mixture in the refrigerator. Arrange 8 bread halves in an overlapping layer over the spinach. Place the remaining 2 bread halves in the center.

3 Whisk the milk, eggs, salt, nutmeg and pepper in a bowl until blended. Pour over the prepared layers. Chill, covered, for 8 to 10 hours.

4 Bake at 350 degrees for 40 minutes. Spoon the reserved mushroom mixture in the center of the strata. Bake for 5 to 10 minutes longer or until the bread is brown.

SERVES 6

SUNDAY BRUNCH STRATA

12 thin slices firm white bread, crusts removed

2 to 3 tablespoons butter or margarine, softened

2 cups thinly sliced yellow onions

8 ounces fresh mushrooms, sliced

½ cup butter or margarine

salt and pepper to taste

1½ pounds bulk mild Italian sausage

12 to 16 ounces Cheddar cheese, shredded

2½ cups milk

5 eggs

1 tablespoon Dijon mustard

1 teaspoon dry mustard

1 teaspoon nutmeg

1 teaspoon salt

⅛ teaspoon pepper

2 tablespoons finely chopped fresh parsley

Great for a large Sunday brunch! Just prepare it the day before, bake at brunch time, and keep warm on a hot tray.

1 Spread the bread slices with 2 to 3 tablespoons butter. Set aside. Sauté the onions and mushrooms in ½ cup butter in a skillet over medium heat for 5 to 8 minutes or until tender. Season with salt and pepper to taste. Brown the sausage in a skillet, stirring until crumbly; drain.

2 Layer the bread, mushroom mixture, sausage and cheese ½ at a time in a greased 7x11-inch or 9x13-inch baking dish. Whisk the milk, eggs, Dijon mustard, dry mustard, nutmeg, 1 teaspoon salt and ⅛ teaspoon pepper in a bowl until blended. Pour over the prepared layers. Chill, covered, for 12 to 24 hours.

3 Sprinkle the parsley over the top. Bake at 350 degrees for 1 hour or until bubbly. Serve immediately with a fruit salad and crusty bread.

SERVES 8

Do you have large wall spaces and no art? Hang a quilt or a beautiful big tapestry for a dramatic visual effect.

SUMMER COTTAGE BREAKFAST PUDDING

1   **(1-pound) loaf firm or dry thinly
sliced white bread**

½   **cup butter, softened**

¾   **cup chopped dried apricots**

½   **cup golden raisins**

¼   **cup dark raisins**

2   **cups milk**

2   **cups whipping cream**

½   **cup sugar**

8   **eggs, beaten**

1   **teaspoon vanilla extract**

1   **teaspoon almond extract**

⅛   **teaspoon salt**

    sugar to taste

Ideal to prepare in advance for a brunch or weekend guests. For an added treat, heat apricot jam with just enough water to make of sauce consistency and stir in a small amount of Grand Marnier to drizzle over the pudding.

1   Spread one side of each bread slice with butter. Cut the slices into halves. Arrange ⅓ of the bread butter side up in a buttered 9x13-inch baking dish.

2   Layer with half the apricots, golden raisins and dark raisins. Arrange half the remaining bread halves in the opposite direction over the prepared layers and top with the remaining apricots, golden raisins and dark raisins. Arrange the remaining bread over the top in the same direction as the first layer.

3   Whisk the milk, whipping cream, ½ cup sugar, eggs, flavorings and salt in a bowl until blended. Pour over the prepared layers. Sprinkle with sugar to taste.

4   Place the baking dish in a larger baking pan. Add enough boiling water to the larger pan to measure 1 inch. Bake at 350 degrees for 1 hour. Serve hot, cold or at room temperature.

SERVES 8 TO 10

TEXAS CORN BREAD

3   (9-ounce) packages corn bread mix

1   pound sausage, cooked, drained

1   pound Cheddar cheese, shredded

1   (16-ounce) can cream-style corn

1½ cups milk

1   (4-ounce) can chopped green chiles

¼   cup chopped onion

3   eggs, beaten

2   tablespoons sugar

1 Combine the corn bread mix, sausage, cheese, corn, milk, chiles, onion, eggs and sugar in a bowl and mix well.

2 Spoon into a greased 9x13-inch baking pan. Bake at 350 degrees for 1 hour.

SERVES 15

Decorating should be a pleasurable pursuit—and not taken too seriously. Every room should have something in it to make guests smile when they enter—an unexpected touch, a hand-crafted pillow, a whimsical object. Even serious rooms can mix light-hearted items with beautiful furnishings. What conversation pieces can set your guests talking? A novelty fabric pillow with faux animals. An appliqué pillow with a bountiful bouquet zig-zag stitched onto a solid-color ground, garlanded with leaves cut from the fabric, and placed just so. A bevy of solid-color silk pillows in vivid colors to add dash to a neutral sofa. A handblown glass vase that picks up the colors of your carpet.

SPINACH QUICHE

1	all ready pie pastry
4	ounces Swiss cheese, shredded
6	slices crisp-fried bacon, drained
8	ounces fresh spinach, trimmed, torn
	salt to taste
1	medium onion, chopped
1	tablespoon butter or margarine
4	eggs
2	cups half-and-half or whipping cream
½	teaspoon salt
¼	teaspoon white pepper
⅛	teaspoon nutmeg

1 Line a 9-inch quiche dish with the pastry, leaving a ½-inch overhang. Fold the edge under to form a standing rim and flute the edge. Bake at 400 degrees for 3 minutes. Prick the bottom of the pastry with a fork. Bake for 5 minutes longer. Cool on a wire rack. Sprinkle the cheese and crumble bacon into the pie shell. Cook the spinach in a small amount of salted water in a 2-quart saucepan for 8 to 10 minutes or until tender; drain. Squeeze the excess moisture from the spinach.

2 Sauté the onion in the butter in a skillet until tender. Whisk the eggs in a bowl until foamy. Stir in the spinach, onion mixture, half-and-half, ½ teaspoon salt, white pepper and nutmeg. Spoon into the prepared pie shell. Bake at 350 degrees for 1 hour or until a knife inserted approximately 1 inch from the center comes out clean. Let stand for 10 minutes before serving.

SERVES 4 TO 6

THE ULTIMATE QUICHE

1	cup shredded Swiss cheese
1	cup shredded medium Cheddar cheese
1	tablespoon flour
1	unbaked (9-inch) pie shell, chilled
1	large onion, thinly sliced
1	cup half-and-half
3	eggs, lightly beaten
¼	teaspoon nutmeg
	salt and pepper to taste
1	(15-ounce) can asparagus tips or fresh asparagus, cut lengthwise into halves

1 Toss the Swiss cheese and Cheddar cheese with the flour in a bowl. Sprinkle into the pie shell. Top with the sliced onion.

2 Heat the half-and-half just to the simmering point in a saucepan. Stir a small amount into the eggs. Stir the eggs into the hot half-and-half. Add the nutmeg, salt and pepper and mix well. Pour over the prepared layers. Arrange the asparagus in a spoke design over the top with the tips to the center.

3 Bake at 425 degrees for 35 minutes or until brown and a knife inserted near the center comes out clean.

SERVES 6

SUPERB CHEESE SOUFFLÉ

3½ tablespoons unsalted butter

3½ tablespoons flour

1½ cups milk

⅓ cup dry white wine

6 egg yolks, slightly beaten

1 tablespoon Dijon mustard

1½ teaspoons fines herbes

2½ cups shredded Swiss or Gruyère cheese

⅛ teaspoon nutmeg

salt and pepper to taste

6 egg whites, at room temperature

⅛ teaspoon cream of tartar

1 Melt the butter in a saucepan over medium heat. Stir in the flour. Cook for 1 minute, stirring constantly. Whisk in the milk gradually. Add the white wine and mix well. Cook just until thickened and smooth, stirring constantly; the mixture will thicken further when the cheese is added. Remove from the heat.

2 Stir a small amount of the hot mixture into the egg yolks. Stir the egg yolks into the hot mixture. Add the Dijon mustard, fines herbes and cheese. Stir in the nutmeg, salt and pepper.

3 Beat the egg whites and cream of tartar in a mixer bowl until stiff but not dry peaks form. Fold into the egg yolk mixture. Spoon into a buttered 2-quart soufflé dish.

4 Bake at 375 degrees for 45 minutes or until puffed and golden brown. Bake at 350 degrees in a convection oven. The soufflé may be tested quickly with a knife to determine doneness without deflating. Serve immediately.

SERVES 6

Designer and author Alexandra Stoddard notes that fresh flowers remind us that life is short and must be cherished. They need not be huge bouquets. An array of single blossoms in small glass flasks will do, or prune flowering trees and bring the branches inside for an early dose of spring color and fragrance. A few real flowers are better than lots of silk or plastic blooms with no fragrance, no life.

SOUFFLÉ ROLL WITH SPINACH FILLING AND TOMATO COULIS

2½ cups milk

½ cup butter

1 cup flour

1 teaspoon salt

¼ teaspoon black pepper

⅛ teaspoon cayenne pepper

10 egg yolks

10 egg whites

2 (10-ounce) packages frozen chopped spinach

¼ cup minced shallots or onion

3 tablespoons butter

8 ounces mushrooms, sliced

1 teaspoon dry mustard

¾ teaspoon salt

¾ teaspoon black pepper

⅛ teaspoon cayenne pepper

12 ounces cream cheese, softened

1 tablespoon lemon juice

Tomato Coulis

This dish does take some time to prepare, but it can be made a day in advance, and the end result is well worth the trouble! The combination of colors makes it a very attractive entrée for brunch or Christmas morning.

1 Grease a 10x15x1-inch baking pan and line with waxed paper or baking parchment. Grease the waxed paper or baking parchment.

2 Heat the milk in a small saucepan. Melt ½ cup butter in a medium saucepan. Stir in the flour, 1 teaspoon salt, ¼ teaspoon black pepper and ⅛ teaspoon cayenne pepper. Cook over low heat for 2 to 3 minutes, stirring constantly. Whisk in the hot milk gradually. Bring to a boil, stirring constantly and reduce the heat. Simmer for 1 minute, stirring frequently.

3 Beat the egg yolks in a bowl until blended. Whisk some of the hot milk mixture into the egg yolks. Whisk the egg yolks into the hot milk mixture. Cook for 1 minute, whisking constantly; do not boil. Let stand until room temperature.

4 Beat the egg whites in a mixer bowl until stiff but not dry peaks form. Whisk ¼ of the egg whites into the egg yolk mixture. Fold the remaining egg whites into the yolk mixture. Spread evenly in the prepared pan.

5 Bake at 325 degrees for 25 minutes. Cover an additional 10x15-inch pan or large wire rack with a dish towel and top with waxed paper. Invert the soufflé immediately onto the waxed paper. Peel off the waxed paper lining the bottom of the soufflé. Roll from the long side as for a jelly roll in the towel. Let stand until cool.

6 Microwave the spinach in a microwave-safe dish just until thawed. Microwave for 1 minute longer; drain and squeeze out the excess moisture.

7 Sauté the shallots in 3 tablespoons butter in a skillet for 1 minute. Add the mushrooms. Cook until the mushrooms are tender and the liquid has evaporated, stirring constantly. Stir in the spinach, dry mustard, ¾ teaspoon salt, ¾ teaspoon black pepper and ⅛ teaspoon cayenne pepper. Cook for 1 minute, stirring constantly. Remove from the heat. Stir in the cream cheese and lemon juice. Let stand until room temperature.

8 Unroll the soufflé roll gently. Spread with the spinach mixture and roll to enclose the filling. Place the roll in a lightly buttered baking pan. Bake, covered tightly with foil, at 325 degrees for 15 to 20 minutes.

9 Reheat the Tomato Coulis in a saucepan. Arrange the roll on a serving platter. Cut into 1-inch slices. Drizzle some of the Tomato Coulis around and over the slices. Serve with the remaining Tomato Coulis.

SERVES 10 TO 14

Tomato Coulis

4	**pounds fresh tomatoes**
2	**cups minced onions**
¼	**cup finely minced shallots**
¼	**cup olive oil**
1¼	**teaspoons salt**
½	**teaspoon Tabasco sauce**
2	**teaspoons minced fresh basil or tarragon, or ¾ teaspoon dried basil or tarragon**

1 Peel and seed the tomatoes; cut into ½-inch pieces. Sauté the onions and shallots in the olive oil in a saucepan over medium heat for 10 to 15 minutes or until tender but not brown. Increase the heat to high and cook for 5 minutes or until the the juices evaporate, stirring frequently.

2 Add the tomatoes, salt and Tabasco sauce and mix well. Bring to a boil. Boil for 10 to 12 minutes or until the excess liquid has evaporated, stirring occasionally. Remove from the heat. Stir in the basil. Let stand until cool.

MAKES 3½ TO 4 CUPS

STRAWBERRY ALMOND FRENCH CREPES

5   **eggs**

2   **cups sifted flour**

2   **tablespoons confectioners' sugar**

1/8   **teaspoon salt**

2   **cups milk**

2   **tablespoons brandy (optional)**

1   **to 2 tablespoons butter**

12   **ounces cream cheese, softened**

1/4   **cup sugar**

3   **tablespoons lemon juice**

1½   **tablespoons grated lemon peel**

     Strawberry Almond Sauce

Serve with sliced oranges, Canadian bacon, Champagne, and coffee at your next brunch. These crepes may be prepared, filled, and stored in the refrigerator one day in advance and baked just before serving time. Prepare the Strawberry Almond Sauce a few hours before the guests arrive.

1   Beat the eggs in a bowl. Sift in the flour, confectioners' sugar and salt; mix well. Add the milk and brandy gradually, stirring until blended.

2   Heat a 7-inch skillet or crepe pan over medium heat. Coat the skillet lightly with the butter. Pour about 2 tablespoons of the batter at a time into the hot skillet, tilting the skillet to spread the batter evenly. Bake until brown on both sides, turning once. Stack the crepes between sheets of waxed paper.

3   Beat the cream cheese, sugar, lemon juice and lemon peel in a mixer bowl until light and fluffy, scraping the bowl occasionally. Spoon 2 tablespoons of the cream cheese mixture in the center of each crepe and roll to enclose the filling. Arrange seam side down in a shallow baking dish. Chill, covered, in the refrigerator until just before baking.

4   Bake at 400 degrees just until heated through. Drizzle with the Strawberry Almond Sauce.

MAKES 8 (2-CREPE) SERVINGS

Strawberry Almond Sauce

2   **cups sweetened sliced strawberries**

1/4   **cup slivered almonds**

1   **tablespoon lemon juice**

1/4   **teaspoon almond extract**

1   Combine the strawberries, almonds, lemon juice and flavoring in a bowl and mix gently. Serve either heated or chilled.

MAKES 2¼ CUPS

SCRAMBLED EGG BRUNCH CREPES

8   **eggs, beaten**

¼   **cup milk**

1   **tablespoon chopped fresh chives**

½   **teaspoon salt**

2   **tablespoons butter**

8   **(6-inch) crepes**

2   **tablespoons butter**

2   **tablespoons flour**

¼   **teaspoon salt**

⅛   **teaspoon pepper**

¾   **cup milk**

¼   **cup shredded Monterey Jack cheese**

¼   **cup dry sherry**

2   **tablespoons grated Parmesan cheese**

Use a basic nondessert crepe recipe or buy prepackaged frozen crepes.

1   Whisk the eggs, ¼ cup milk, chives and ½ teaspoon salt in a bowl. Cook in 2 tablespoons butter in a skillet until set, stirring frequently. Spoon ¼ cup of the eggs into the center of each crepe; fold the sides to the center to enclose the filling. Arrange seam side down in a 7x12-inch baking dish.

2   Melt 2 tablespoons butter in a saucepan. Stir in the flour, ¼ teaspoon salt and pepper. Add ¾ cup milk and mix well. Cook until thickened and bubbly, stirring constantly. Stir in the Monterey Jack cheese, sherry and Parmesan cheese. Spoon over the crepes.

3   Bake, covered, at 375 degrees for 20 to 25 minutes or until bubbly.

4   The crepes may be prepared 1 day in advance, adding the sauce just before baking.

SERVES 8

Upholsterers can work magic on tired, worn chairs and sofas; if necessary, they literally rebuild the piece from the frame out. And if it's not worth recovering, Calico Corners offers over 200 furniture frames to be custom-covered in your choice of fabric and styling. Add a contrast welt; ruffle the skirt; fringe the pillows; use a mix of fabrics—detail it just the way you want.

FAMOUS BUTTERMILK PANCAKES

2	cups flour
3	tablespoons sugar
2	teaspoons baking powder
1	teaspoon baking soda
½	teaspoon salt
2	cups buttermilk
2	eggs, beaten
2	tablespoons vegetable oil
	milk (optional)

These pancakes bring back happy memories of mornings around the kitchen table. They're almost as quick to make as anything out of a package—and so much better!

1   Mix the flour, sugar, baking powder, baking soda and salt in a bowl. Add the buttermilk, eggs and oil and mix just until moistened. Add a small amount of milk if a thinner batter is preferred.

2   Pour approximately ¼ cup of the batter at a time onto a hot lightly buttered griddle or into a skillet. Bake until bubbles appear on the surface and the underside is golden brown. Turn the pancake over and bake until golden brown.

MAKES 6 TO 8 PANCAKES

FABULOUS FRENCH TOAST

5	eggs
⅔	cup whipping cream
⅓	cup Triple Sec
2	tablespoons sugar
	grated zest of 1 orange
2	teaspoons cinnamon
12	slices dry French bread
6	tablespoons unsalted butter
	confectioners' sugar

1   Whisk the eggs and whipping cream in a shallow dish until blended. Whisk in the Triple Sec, sugar, orange zest and cinnamon.

2   Dip the bread slices in the egg mixture, coating well. Heat 3 tablespoons of the butter in a skillet until melted. Add 6 of the bread slices. Cook until brown on both sides, turning once or twice. Remove the slices to a baking sheet. Keep warm in a 200-degree oven. Repeat the procedure with the remaining butter and bread slices. Sprinkle with confectioners' sugar just before serving.

MAKES 12 SLICES

GINGERBREAD WAFFLES

½ cup boiling water or coffee

⅓ cup vegetable shortening

½ cup dark molasses

⅓ cup packed dark brown sugar

1 cup plus 2 tablespoons flour

1¼ teaspoons baking powder

1 teaspoon ginger

¾ teaspoon cinnamon

¼ teaspoon baking soda

¼ teaspoon ground cloves

¼ teaspoon nutmeg

1 egg, beaten

Lemon Sauce

Make extra waffles to freeze and reheat in the toaster or oven.

1 Combine the boiling water and shortening in a bowl, stirring until the shortening melts. Add the molasses and brown sugar and mix well. Cool to room temperature.

2 Mix the flour, baking powder, ginger, cinnamon, baking soda, cloves and nutmeg in a mixer bowl. Add the egg and shortening mixture. Beat until smooth, scraping the bowl occasionally.

3 Bake in a waffle iron using manufacturer's directions; waffles become crisp as they cool. Serve with Lemon Sauce.

MAKES 4 TO 6 WAFFLES

Lemon Sauce

½ cup sugar

1 tablespoon cornstarch

⅛ teaspoon salt

1 cup boiling water

3 tablespoons lemon juice

2 tablespoons margarine or butter

1 teaspoon grated lemon peel

1 Combine the sugar, cornstarch and salt in a saucepan and mix well. Stir in the boiling water gradually. Cook for 5 minutes or until thickened, stirring constantly.

2 Remove from the heat and stir in the lemon juice, margarine and lemon peel.

MAKES 1¼ CUPS

SOUTHERN-STYLE BISCUITS

2   cups flour
1   tablespoon baking powder
1   teaspoon salt
¼   cup unsalted butter
¾   to 1 cup buttermilk

1 Mix the flour, baking powder and salt in a bowl. Cut in the butter until crumbly. Add the buttermilk, stirring just until moistened.

2 Shape by hand or roll the dough ¼ inch thick on a lightly floured surface and cut with a biscuit cutter.

3 Arrange the biscuits with sides touching on a baking sheet. Bake at 350 degrees for 8 minutes or until light brown.

MAKES 9 TO 12 BISCUITS

BLUEBERRY BREAKFAST CAKE

2   cups flour
2   teaspoons baking powder
½   teaspoon salt
¾   cup sugar
¼   cup butter, softened
1   egg
½   cup milk
2   cups fresh blueberries
½   cup sugar
⅓   cup flour
½   teaspoon cinnamon
¼   cup butter, softened

1 Sift 2 cups flour, baking powder and salt into a bowl and mix well. Beat ¾ cup sugar, ¼ cup butter and egg in a mixer bowl until creamy, scraping the bowl occasionally. Add the dry ingredients alternately with the milk, mixing well after each addition. Fold in the blueberries. Spoon the batter into a greased 9x9-inch baking pan.

2 Combine ½ cup sugar, ⅓ cup flour and cinnamon in a bowl and mix well. Cut in ¼ cup butter until crumbly. Sprinkle over the batter. Bake at 350 degrees for 40 to 45 minutes or until brown.

SERVES 9

CREAM CHEESE COFFEE CAKE

2 cups flour

2 teaspoons baking powder

½ teaspoon salt

1 egg, beaten

milk

1 cup sugar

6 tablespoons margarine

8 ounces cream cheese, softened

⅔ cup sugar

½ cup sour cream

1 teaspoon vanilla extract

2 eggs

1 cup flour

½ cup sugar

½ cup margarine

1 teaspoon vanilla extract

1 Mix 2 cups flour, baking powder and salt in a bowl. Combine 1 egg with enough milk to measure ¾ cup. Beat 1 cup sugar and 6 tablespoons margarine in a mixer bowl until creamy, scraping the bowl occasionally. Add the dry ingredients alternately with the egg mixture, mixing just until moistened. Spoon the batter into a 9x13-inch baking pan.

2 Beat the cream cheese, ⅔ cup sugar, sour cream, 1 teaspoon vanilla and 2 eggs in a mixer bowl until smooth. Spread over the prepared layer.

3 Mix 1 cup flour and ½ cup sugar in a bowl. Cut in ½ cup margarine and 1 teaspoon vanilla until crumbly. Sprinkle over the top. Bake at 350 degrees for 40 to 50 minutes or until golden brown.

SERVES 15

Put away heavy draperies or bed-hangings for the spring/summer season. Tie up colorful sheers in florals, subtle stripes, madras plaids, or gingham checks. Lavish your windows or bed with lace or light cotton/linen weaves that can billow with the breeze.

APPLE CURRANT MUFFINS

2   **cups flour**

1   **teaspoon baking powder**

½   **teaspoon nutmeg**

⅔   **cup packed brown sugar**

⅔   **cup unsweetened apple juice**

⅓   **cup peanut oil**

1   **egg**

1   **cup finely chopped Granny Smith apple**

½   **cup chopped walnuts or pecans**

½   **cup currants**

1   **teaspoon (or more) cinnamon**

1   Sift the flour, baking powder and nutmeg into a bowl and mix well. Stir in the brown sugar. Whisk the apple juice, peanut oil and egg in a bowl until blended. Add to the flour mixture and mix gently.

2   Mix the apple, walnuts, currants and cinnamon in a bowl. Fold into the batter.

3   Spoon into buttered muffin cups. Bake at 400 degrees for 23 to 25 minutes or until the muffins spring back when touched lightly and are golden brown in color. Serve warm.

MAKES 1 DOZEN

OATMEAL MUFFINS

1   **cup quick-cooking oats**

1   **cup buttermilk**

½   **cup packed brown sugar**

¼   **cup vegetable oil**

1   **egg, beaten**

1   **cup sifted flour**

2   **teaspoons baking powder**

½   **teaspoon baking soda**

½   **teaspoon salt**

½   **teaspoon cinnamon**

1   Combine the oats, buttermilk and brown sugar in a bowl and mix well. Let stand for 10 minutes. Stir in the oil and egg.

2   Sift the flour, baking powder, baking soda, salt and cinnamon into a bowl and mix well. Add to the oats mixture, stirring just until moistened. Fill 2½-inch muffins cups ⅔ full.

3   Bake at 375 degrees for 25 minutes or until a wooden pick inserted in the center comes out clean. Add raisins or chopped nuts with the dry ingredients if desired.

MAKES 1 DOZEN

GRANDMA'S CINNAMON ROLLS

1½ cups boiling water

1 cup evaporated milk, at room temperature

½ cup sugar

½ cup canola oil

3 envelopes dry yeast

1 tablespoon salt

6 to 7½ cups flour

2 tablespoons melted butter

2½ cups sugar

1 cup packed brown sugar

2 tablespoons cinnamon

1 (1-pound) package confectioners' sugar

½ cup plus 2 tablespoons milk

2 teaspoons vanilla extract

1 Combine the boiling water, evaporated milk, ½ cup sugar and oil in a bowl and mix well. Sprinkle with the yeast. Let stand for about 5 minutes or until bubbly and mix well. Add the salt and 6 heaping cups of the flour and mix well. Add additional flour if the dough is too sticky.

2 Knead the dough on a floured surface for 8 to 10 minutes or until smooth and elastic. Place in a greased bowl, turning to coat the surface. Let rise, covered, in a warm place for 1½ hours or until doubled in bulk; dough is ready if an indentation remains when touched.

3 Punch the dough down and divide into 2 equal portions. Roll each portion into a 10x12-inch rectangle on a lightly floured surface. Spread with the melted butter. Sprinkle with a mixture of 2½ cups sugar, brown sugar and cinnamon. Roll from the wide side to enclose the filling; pinch the edges to seal. Cut each roll into 12 slices.

4 Arrange the slices slightly apart in 2 greased 9x13-inch baking pans. Let rise, covered, in a warm place for 30 minutes or until doubled in bulk.

5 Bake at 350 degrees for 20 to 25 minutes or until golden brown. Spread the warm rolls with a mixture of the confectioners' sugar, milk and vanilla.

MAKES 2 DOZEN

Doesn't everyone need more storage space? Consider a storage ottoman for kids' games, toys, magazines, and craft or needlework projects. The top lifts to reveal a recess of storage space that can roll around with you.

ORANGE POPPY SEED SCONES

2¼ cups flour

½ cup sugar

¼ cup poppy seeds

1 teaspoon cream of tartar

¾ teaspoon baking soda

½ teaspoon salt

½ cup unsalted butter, cut into ½-inch cubes, chilled

¼ cup orange juice

1 egg

¼ teaspoon grated orange peel

1 egg white

½ teaspoon water

These scones are perfect with tea or cappuccino.

1 Butter a 10-inch circle in the center of a baking sheet. Mix the flour, sugar, poppy seeds, cream of tartar, baking soda and salt in a bowl. Cut in the butter with a pastry blender or 2 knives until crumbly. Whisk the orange juice, egg and orange peel in a bowl. Add to the flour mixture and mix well; dough will be sticky.

2 Pat with floured hands into a 9-inch circle on the prepared baking sheet. Brush with a mixture of the egg white and water. Cut the circle into 8 wedges with a serrated knife.

3 Bake at 375 degrees for 20 to 25 minutes or until a wooden pick inserted in the center comes out clean and the top is light brown. Cool on the baking sheet on a wire rack for 5 minutes. Remove to a wire rack. Serve warm or at room temperature. Store in an airtight container.

MAKES 8 SCONES

LEMON BREAD

1½ cups sifted flour

1 teaspoon each baking powder and salt

1 cup sugar

⅓ cup melted butter

3 tablespoons lemon extract

2 eggs

½ cup milk

½ cup chopped pecans

1½ tablespoons grated lemon peel

½ cup sugar

¼ cup lemon juice

1 Sift the flour, baking powder and salt into a bowl and mix well. Beat 1 cup sugar, butter and flavoring in a mixer bowl until blended. Beat in the eggs. Add the flour mixture alternately with the milk, beating just until blended. Fold in the pecans and lemon peel.

2 Spoon the batter into a greased and floured 5x9-inch loaf pan. Bake at 350 degrees for 1 hour or until a wooden pick inserted in the center comes out clean. Cool in the pan on a wire rack for 10 minutes. Invert onto a wire rack.

3 Drizzle the warm loaf with a mixture of ½ cup sugar and lemon juice. Let stand until cool. Store, wrapped in foil, at room temperature for 24 hours before serving.

SERVES 10

STRAWBERRY BREAD

- 3 cups sifted flour
- 1 teaspoon salt
- 1 teaspoon cream of tartar
- ½ teaspoon baking soda
- 1 cup strawberry jam
- ½ cup sour cream
- 1 cup chopped walnuts
- 1½ cups sugar
- 1 cup butter or margarine
- 1 teaspoon vanilla extract
- ¼ teaspoon lemon extract
- 4 eggs

1 Sift the flour, salt, cream of tartar and baking soda together. Combine the jam and sour cream in a bowl. Add the dry ingredients and walnuts and mix well.

2 Beat the sugar, butter and flavorings in a mixer bowl until creamy, scraping the bowl occasionally. Beat in the eggs 1 at a time. Stir into the flour mixture.

3 Spoon the batter into 2 greased and floured 5x9-inch loaf pans. Bake at 350 degrees for 50 to 60 minutes or until a wooden pick inserted in the center comes out clean. Cool in the pans on a wire rack for 5 minutes. Invert onto a wire rack to cool completely.

MAKES 2 LOAVES

JALAPEÑO CORN BREAD

- 1 cup cornmeal
- ½ cup flour
- 2 teaspoons baking powder
- ½ teaspoon salt
- 1 cup milk
- ¼ cup vegetable oil
- 2 eggs, beaten
- 2 teaspoons molasses
- 1 cup whole kernel corn
- 1 cup shredded sharp Cheddar cheese
- 1 onion, grated
- 2 jalapeño peppers, chopped

1 Heat an oiled 8x8-inch baking pan at 375 degrees until smoking.

2 Combine the cornmeal, flour, baking powder and salt in a bowl and mix well. Stir in the milk, oil, eggs and molasses. Add the corn, cheese, onion and jalapeño peppers and mix well.

3 Spoon the batter into the prepared baking pan. Bake for 40 minutes or until brown and crisp. Serve immediately.

SERVES 6 TO 8

SPICED-UP PECANS

2	tablespoons butter
1	tablespoon olive oil
1	tablespoon Worcestershire sauce
½	to 1 teaspoon Tabasco sauce
¾	teaspoon ground cumin
½	to 1 teaspoon paprika
½	to 1 teaspoon garlic powder
2	cups pecan halves
2	teaspoons coarse salt

Spice up these pecans to your individual taste by varying the amounts of the seasonings used.

1 Melt the butter with the olive oil in a saucepan over low heat. Add the Worcestershire sauce, Tabasco sauce, cumin, paprika and garlic powder and mix well. Cook for 2 to 3 minutes, stirring frequently.

2 Add the pecans and toss to coat well. Spread on a baking sheet. Bake at 325 degrees for 15 minutes, shaking occasionally. Sprinkle with salt and toss to coat evenly.

3 Let stand on baking sheet until cool. Store in an airtight container.

MAKES 2 CUPS

ARTICHOKE CHEESE SQUARES

3	slices bacon, chopped
1	medium onion, chopped
1	garlic clove, chopped
4	eggs, beaten
1	(15-ounce) can artichoke hearts, drained, chopped
8	ounces Swiss cheese, shredded
¼	cup bread crumbs
	oregano to taste

This is a great dish to transport to a party. Bake it at home and reheat it in the microwave just before serving.

1 Fry the bacon with the onion and garlic in a skillet until the bacon is crisp; drain. Combine with the eggs, artichokes, cheese, bread crumbs and oregano in a bowl and mix well.

2 Spoon into a greased 9x13-inch baking pan. Bake at 375 degrees for 25 to 30 minutes or until set. Let stand for 5 minutes before cutting into squares to serve.

3 You may substitute shrimp or crab meat for the artichokes.

MAKES 36 SQUARES

CRAB DE JONGE

¼ **cup chopped onion**

1 **tablespoon butter**

1 **teaspoon olive oil**

2 **cups concentrated fish stock or clam juice**

½ **cup white wine**

1 **bunch fresh dillweed, trimmed, chopped**

1 **tomato, peeled, seeded, chopped**

1 **teaspoon butter, softened**

1 **teaspoon flour**

1 **pound lump crab meat**

1 **tablespoon Mustard Butter**

6 **ounces Gruyère cheese, shredded**

1 Sauté the onion in a mixture of 1 tablespoon butter and olive oil in a skillet until tender. Add the stock and white wine and mix well.

2 Cook until slightly reduced, stirring constantly. Stir in the dillweed and tomato. Cook for 1 minute, stirring constantly. Stir in a mixture of 1 teaspoon butter and flour. Cook until slightly thickened, stirring constantly.

3 Place the crab meat in six 3- or 4-inch ramekins. Spoon the stock mixture over the crab meat. Top each serving with about ½ teaspoon of the Mustard Butter. Sprinkle with the cheese. Bake at 500 degrees until golden brown.

SERVES 6

Mustard Butter

¼ **cup butter, softened**

¼ **cup Dijon mustard**

1 Mix the butter and Dijon mustard in a bowl until blended.

2 Store, covered, in the refrigerator.

MAKES ½ CUP

DIM SUM DUMPLINGS

1   cup chopped carrot

2   green onions, chopped

1   pound ground chicken

1   tablespoon light soy sauce

2   teaspoons dry sherry

1   teaspoon sesame oil

1   teaspoon Chinese chili sauce

¼   teaspoon salt

30   round won ton wrappers

¼   cup vegetable oil

   Spinach Dressing

1   tablespoon white sesame seeds, toasted

1 Mince the carrot and green onions coarsely in a food processor. Combine with the chicken, soy sauce, sherry, sesame oil, chili sauce and salt in a bowl and mix well.

2 Spoon 2 teaspoons of the chicken mixture into the center of each won ton wrapper. Moisten the edges of the wrappers with water and fold over to enclose the filling; press the edges to seal. Moisten the ends of the dumplings and press the moistened ends together; dumplings should look like caps. Arrange on a baking sheet coated generously with the oil. Chill for up to 5 hours or freeze.

3 Cook in boiling water to cover in a stockpot for for 3 minutes or until the dumplings float to the surface. Remove gently to a colander to drain.

4 Arrange on a heated serving plate; drizzle with the Spinach Dressing and sprinkle with the sesame seeds. Serve immediately.

SERVES 6 TO 8

Spinach Dressing

12   ounces fresh spinach, trimmed

¼   cup chopped fresh cilantro

8   basil leaves

1   green onion

2   garlic cloves

2   teaspoons minced fresh gingerroot

1   teaspoon grated orange peel

2   tablespoons each dry sherry, white vinegar and sesame oil

1   tablespoon light soy sauce

2   teaspoons each hoisin sauce and sugar

½   teaspoon Chinese chili sauce

1 Process the spinach in a food processor until finely minced. Add the cilantro, basil, green onion, garlic, gingerroot and orange peel. Process until finely minced.

2 Add the sherry, vinegar, sesame oil, soy sauce, hoisin sauce, sugar and chili sauce. Process for 1 minute. Process for 20 seconds longer or until puréed.

MAKES 1½ CUPS

HAM ROLL-UPS

4	ounces cream cheese with chives, softened
½	cup chopped marinated artichoke hearts, drained
2	tablespoons minced pimento
3	flour tortillas
6	thin slices ham
6	thin slices provolone cheese

1 Mix the cream cheese, artichoke hearts and pimento in a bowl. Spread over 1 side of each tortilla. Top with the ham. Arrange the sliced cheese down the center of each tortilla. Roll to enclose the filling.

2 Wrap individually in plastic wrap. Chill for 8 to 10 hours. Cut into 1-inch slices. Serve immediately.

SERVES 4

SHRIMP STRUDEL

1½	cups shredded Swiss cheese
4	ounces chopped steamed shrimp or crab meat
½	cup sour cream
¼	cup thinly sliced green onions
1	egg, beaten
1	sheet frozen puff pastry, thawed

1 Combine the cheese, shrimp, sour cream, green onions and ½ of the egg in a bowl and mix well. Roll the puff pastry into a 10x18-inch rectangle on a lightly floured surface. Spread the shrimp mixture lengthwise over ½ of the rectangle. Brush the edges of the pastry with some of the remaining egg. Fold the pastry over to enclose the filling and press the edges with a fork to seal.

2 Arrange the pastry on a baking sheet. Brush with the remaining egg. Bake at 400 degrees for 20 to 25 minutes. Let stand for 20 minutes before slicing to serve.

SERVES 6 TO 8

MARINATED SHRIMP

1   garlic clove, cut into halves

2   pounds cooked shrimp, peeled, deveined, patted dry

½   cup chopped celery

1   scallion, chopped

1   tablespoon chopped fresh chives

6   tablespoons olive oil

3   tablespoons lemon juice

2   tablespoons chili sauce

2   tablespoons catsup

2   tablespoons horseradish

1   tablespoon prepared mustard

¾   teaspoon salt

¼   teaspoon paprika

¼   teaspoon Tabasco sauce

1   Rub a large bowl with the garlic. Add the shrimp, celery, scallion and chives and mix well. Combine the the olive oil, lemon juice, chili sauce, catsup, horseradish, mustard, salt, paprika and Tabasco sauce in a small bowl and mix well. Add to the shrimp mixture and mix gently.

2   Marinate, covered, in the refrigerator for 6 to 12 hours, stirring occasionally; drain. Serve with wooden picks.

SERVES 10 TO 12

SPINACH AND CHEESE SQUARES

1   cup flour

1   teaspoon baking soda

1½   teaspoons salt

1   cup milk

3   eggs, beaten

1   pound Swiss cheese, shredded

10   ounces fresh spinach, chopped

1   small onion, minced

½   cup margarine

1   Mix the flour, baking soda and salt in a bowl. Stir in the milk and eggs. Add the cheese, spinach and onion and mix well.

2   Melt the margarine in a 9x13-inch baking pan in a 350-degree oven. Spoon in the spinach mixture. Bake for 30 minutes or until light brown. Cool slightly. Cut into squares.

3   You may substitute two 10-ounce packages drained thawed frozen chopped spinach for the fresh spinach.

MAKES 36 SQUARES

VEGETABLE PIZZA

2	(8-count) cans crescent rolls
6	ounces cream cheese, softened
1	cup mayonnaise
⅔	cup sour cream
2	envelopes ranch salad dressing mix
1	cup chopped broccoli florets
1	cup chopped cauliflowerets
1	cup chopped carrot
1	cup chopped tomato
¼	cup chopped onion
¼	cup chopped red or green bell pepper
	grated Parmesan cheese to taste

1 Unroll the crescent roll dough. Pat over the bottom of a baking sheet, pressing the edges and perforations to seal. Bake at 375 degrees for 11 minutes or until light brown. Let stand until cool.

2 Blend the cream cheese, mayonnaise, sour cream and dressing mix in a bowl. Spread over the baked layer.

3 Combine the broccoli, cauliflower, carrot, tomato, onion and red pepper in a bowl and toss gently. Sprinkle over the cream cheese layer and press lightly. Sprinkle with Parmesan cheese. Chill, covered, until serving time. Cut into bite-size squares.

4 The flavor is enhanced if the pizza is prepared 1 day in advance and stored, covered, in the refrigerator. Vary the vegetables according to your taste.

SERVES 10 TO 12

ZUCCHINI GORGONZOLA ROUNDS

10	small zucchini, cut into ½-inch slices
8	ounces Gorgonzola cheese, chilled, cut into small pieces
2	pints cherry tomatoes, thinly sliced
	small fresh basil leaves
5	ounces Parmesan cheese, finely grated
	freshly ground pepper

1 Scoop out the center of each zucchini slice with a melon baller, leaving the bottom of each slice intact. Layer about ½ teaspoon of the Gorgonzola cheese, 1 cherry tomato slice and 1 basil leaf on each slice. Sprinkle with the Parmesan cheese and pepper.

2 Arrange the slices on a baking sheet lined with parchment paper. Bake at 400 degrees for 7 to 10 minutes or until the cheese melts; do not brown. Serve immediately. Place on a warm baking stone to serve if desired.

MAKES 40

CAPONATA

½ cup olive oil

1½ pounds unpeeled eggplant, cut into ½-inch pieces

2 large red bell peppers, chopped

1½ cups thinly sliced celery

1 large onion, chopped

3 garlic cloves, minced

1 cup water

1 cup sliced black olives

¼ cup tomato paste

¼ cup red wine vinegar

2 tablespoons coarsely chopped fresh basil, or 1 teaspoon dried basil

1 tablespoon sugar

1 tablespoon drained capers

¼ cup pine nuts

A traditional Sicilian/Italian dish that is a little time-consuming to prepare, but well worth the effort if you love eggplant.

1 Heat the olive oil in a large skillet over medium heat until hot. Add the eggplant. Cook, covered, for 5 minutes or just until tender, stirring occasionally; remove the cover. Cook for 10 minutes longer or until the eggplant begins to brown, stirring frequently.

2 Stir in the bell peppers, celery, onion and garlic. Cook for 6 to 8 minutes or until the onion is tender, stirring frequently. Add the water, black olives, tomato paste, wine vinegar, basil, sugar and capers and mix well. Cook for 10 minutes longer or until thickened, stirring frequently. Store, covered, for up to 1 week at this point if desired.

3 Toast the pine nuts in a skillet over medium heat for 5 minutes or until light brown, stirring frequently. Sprinkle over the caponata. Serve at room temperature.

MAKES 1½ QUARTS

Layer up for fall: add a chenille throw or two to sofas and reading chairs; line it with a damask, plaid, or brushed cotton fabric for extra softness.

ITALIAN SALSA

- **10** plum tomatoes, chopped
- **½** cup chopped fresh basil
- **¼** cup olive oil
- **1** garlic clove, minced
- **2** tablespoons grated Parmesan cheese
- **1** tablespoon finely chopped onion
- **2** teaspoons balsamic vinegar
- **1** teaspoon salt
- **¼** teaspoon pepper

All ingredients in this dish can be adjusted, so experiment with a version to suit your taste.

1   Mix the tomatoes, basil, olive oil, garlic, cheese, onion, balsamic vinegar, salt and pepper in a bowl.

2   Serve on toasted thin slices of Italian bread, crackers or bagels.

SERVES 20

BLACK BEAN SALSA

- **1** (15-ounce) can black beans, rinsed, drained
- **½** cup cooked fresh corn kernels
- **2** tomatoes, cut into ¼-inch pieces
- **1** each red and green bell pepper, cut into ¼-inch pieces
- **½** cup chopped red onion
- **1** jalapeño pepper, sliced (optional)
- **⅓** cup fresh lime juice
- **⅓** cup extra-virgin olive oil
- **⅓** cup chopped fresh coriander
- **1** teaspoon salt
- **½** teaspoon cumin
- **½** teaspoon ground red chiles, or ⅛ teaspoon cayenne pepper

1   Combine the beans, corn, tomatoes, red pepper, green pepper, red onion and jalapeño pepper in a bowl and mix gently.

2   Mix the lime juice, olive oil, coriander, salt, cumin and chiles in a small bowl. Add to the bean mixture and mix gently. Let stand at room temperature to blend the flavors before serving or store, covered, in the refrigerator for 24 hours; bring to room temperature before serving.

SERVES 8 TO 10

TOMATO BRUSCHETTA

3   large tomatoes, chopped

1   small red onion, finely chopped

2   tablespoons chopped roasted red bell
    pepper

1   garlic clove, minced

2   tablespoons chopped fresh basil

2   tablespoons balsamic vinegar

5   tablespoons extra-virgin olive oil

    salt and freshly ground pepper
    to taste

1   loaf Italian bread, cut into
    1-inch slices

    grated pecorino Romano cheese

1   Combine the tomatoes, red onion, red pepper, garlic, basil, balsamic vinegar and 1 tablespoon of the olive oil in a bowl and mix gently. Season with salt and pepper. Let stand at room temperature for 1 hour or longer. Store, covered, in the refrigerator for up to 4 days if desired. Bring to room temperature before serving.

2   Brush both sides of each bread slice with the remaining olive oil. Grill over medium-hot coals until brown on both sides. Arrange the slices on a serving platter. Spoon some of the tomato topping onto the center of each slice and sprinkle with cheese.

SERVES 6

Make new pillows for spring. When pillow covers are made with ties or zippers, they can easily be slipped over their fall/winter covers beneath. If bright colors are not the ticket, consider fresh florals and lively solids in warm corals, spring greens, azure blues, or raspberry pinks. Even printed sheers and laces can be layered over other fabrics to create unique pillows.

MIDDLE EASTERN EGGPLANT DIP

1   large eggplant

1   garlic clove, crushed

½   teaspoon salt

3   tablespoons tahini

     juice of 1 lemon

3   tablespoons cold water

2   tablespoons chopped fresh parsley

     hot Hungarian paprika to taste

     olive oil to taste

1   Prick the eggplant 3 or 4 times with a wooden pick and place on a baking sheet. Bake at 350 degrees until the eggplant collapses. Let stand until cool. Chop the eggplant, discarding the skin and seeds. Squeeze to remove any bitter juices.

2   Mix the garlic and salt in a bowl. Combine the garlic mixture, tahini and lemon juice in a food processor container. Process until blended. Add the cold water and eggplant. Process until blended.

3   Spoon into a serving bowl. Sprinkle with the parsley and paprika. Drizzle with olive oil. Serve with pita wedges.

SERVES 6 TO 8

COWBOY CAVIAR

2   tablespoons red wine vinegar

1½ to 2 teaspoons hot sauce

1½ teaspoons vegetable oil

1   garlic clove, minced

⅛   teaspoon pepper

1   firm ripe avocado, cut into ½-inch pieces

8   ounces Roma tomatoes, chopped

1   (15-ounce) can black-eyed peas, rinsed, drained

1   (11-ounce) can corn kernels, rinsed, drained

⅔   cup sliced green onions

⅔   cup chopped cilantro or basil

     salt to taste

Add shredded cabbage to Cowboy Caviar to serve it as a salad.

1   Whisk the wine vinegar, hot sauce, oil, garlic and pepper in a bowl. Add the avocado and toss gently to coat.

2   Stir in the tomatoes, peas, corn, green onions and cilantro. Season with salt. Serve with tortilla chips.

SERVES 10 TO 12

SAUSALITO CRAB DIP

1½ cups sour cream

1 envelope leek soup mix

1 tablespoon lemon juice

⅛ teaspoon Tabasco sauce

1 (14-ounce) can artichoke hearts, chopped

1 (6-ounce) package frozen crab meat, thawed, drained, chopped

1 cup shredded Swiss cheese

1 tablespoon chopped fresh dillweed, or 1 teaspoon dried dillweed

1 Combine the sour cream, soup mix, lemon juice and Tabasco sauce in a bowl and mix well. Stir in the artichokes, crab meat, Swiss cheese and dillweed.

2 Chill, covered, for 2 hours or longer before serving. Serve with assorted party crackers, pita wedges or party bread.

SERVES 20

HOT ARTICHOKE SPREAD

2 (14-ounce) cans water-pack artichoke hearts, drained

1 cup grated Parmesan cheese

1 cup mayonnaise

1 drop of hot pepper sauce

1 small garlic clove, minced

1 teaspoon lemon juice

1 Process the artichokes, cheese, mayonnaise, hot pepper sauce, garlic and lemon juice in a food processor until smooth. Spoon into a 1½-quart baking dish sprayed with nonstick cooking spray.

2 Bake at 350 degrees for 30 minutes or until light brown and bubbly. Serve with party rye bread.

SERVES 10 TO 12

SHRIMP PÂTÉ

2   tablespoons chopped fresh dillweed,
     or 1 scant teaspoon dried dillweed

1   tablespoon chopped shallot

4   ounces cream cheese, softened

3   tablespoons mayonnaise

½   cup peeled steamed small shrimp

     lemon juice to taste

1 Mince the dillweed and shallot in a food processor. Add the cream cheese and mayonnaise. Process until smooth. Add the shrimp. Process just until mixed. Stir in lemon juice to taste.

2 Chill, covered, for several hours before serving. Serve with assorted party crackers.

SERVES 4 TO 6

TUNA PÂTÉ

5   slices crisp-fried bacon

16   ounces cream cheese, chopped,
     softened

2   (7-ounce) cans water-pack white
     tuna, drained

2   tablespoons lemon juice

2   tablespoons chopped fresh parsley

1   tablespoon soy sauce

1   tablespoon pickle juice

     chopped celery to taste

1   slice black olive

1 Reserve 1 slice of the bacon. Crumble the remaining bacon. Combine the crumbled bacon, cream cheese, tuna, lemon juice, parsley, soy sauce, pickle juice and celery in a bowl and mix well.

2 Pack into an oiled fish mold or 3-cup bowl. Invert onto a lettuce-lined serving platter. Decorate with an olive slice for the eye and the reserved bacon slice for the gills. Serve with assorted party crackers.

SERVES 16 TO 20

BLEU CHEESE FLAN

¾ cup butter cracker crumbs

2 tablespoons melted margarine

16 ounces cream cheese, softened

8 ounces bleu cheese, crumbled

⅔ cup sour cream

3 eggs

1 tablespoon sugar

⅛ teaspoon pepper

1 cup sour cream

orange or lemon yogurt to taste (optional)

This flan may be prepared several days in advance and stored, covered, in the refrigerator or frozen for future use.

1 Toss the cracker crumbs and margarine in a bowl. Pat over the bottom of a 9-inch springform pan. Bake at 350 degrees for 10 minutes.

2 Beat the cream cheese and bleu cheese in a mixer bowl until blended. Add ⅔ cup sour cream, eggs, sugar and pepper. Beat until smooth. Spoon into the prepared springform pan. Bake at 300 degrees for 45 minutes.

3 Blend 1 cup sour cream and yogurt in a small bowl. Spread over the flan. Bake for 10 minutes longer. Cool in the pan on a wire rack. Remove to a serving platter. Serve with sliced fresh fruit, assorted party crackers and/or sliced French bread.

SERVES 16 TO 20

Haven't we all made a color mistake when painting? Here's how to avoid surprises: select your color and then buy a quart (or the smallest quantity) of that paint. Apply it to a big sheet of white posterboard and tack it to the walls of your room. Live with it for a day or two, by daylight and evening light, and see how it works with your furnishings. Posterboard can be moved from wall to wall, if desired, or contrasted with woodwork. If you've chosen the wrong color, a quart of paint is a small loss.

HOLIDAY EGGNOG

6   egg yolks

½   cup sugar, or to taste

¾   to 1½ cups bourbon

¼   to ½ cup rum

¼   to ½ cup brandy or Cointreau

2   teaspoons vanilla extract

3   cups whipping cream

2   cups milk

6   egg whites

3   tablespoons sugar

    nutmeg to taste

Delicious but volatile, even with the smaller amounts of spirits.

1   Beat the egg yolks in a mixer bowl until blended. Add ½ cup sugar gradually, beating constantly until light and fluffy. Add the bourbon, rum and brandy gradually, beating constantly until blended. Stir in the vanilla.

2   Chill, covered, for 1 hour or longer, stirring in about ⅓ of the whipping cream and ⅓ of the milk every 30 minutes until all are used, mixing well and chilling after each addition.

3   Beat the egg whites at serving time in a mixer bowl until stiff peaks form. Fold half the egg whites into the egg mixture. Pour the eggnog into a punch bowl. Beat 3 tablespoons sugar into the remaining egg whites. Spoon onto the punch and swirl or drop by spoonfuls over individual servings. Sprinkle with nutmeg.

MAKES 20 TO 25 (½-CUP) SERVINGS

YOGI TEA

2   quarts water

15   whole cloves

20   green cardamom pods, crushed

20   whole black peppercorns

3   cinnamon sticks, broken

8   slices fresh gingerroot

½   teaspoon black tea

3   cups milk or soy milk

    honey or maple syrup (optional)

Yogi Tea, from a recipe by Yogi Bhajan, carries healing benefits. The black tea is the necessary catalyst to the recipe; herbal teas and refined sugar counteract its effect, but honey or maple syrup can be used to sweeten the tea.

1   Bring the water, cloves, cardamom, peppercorns, cinnamon sticks and gingerroot to a boil in a large saucepan; reduce the heat. Simmer, covered, for 2 to 3 hours. Stir in the tea and remove from the heat.

2   Let stand to steep for 2 to 3 minutes. Add the milk. Cook just until heated through; do not boil. Strain and stir in honey or maple syrup to sweeten. Pour into mugs.

SERVES 8 TO 10

FRUIT SHAKE

1   cup low-fat plain yogurt

1   cup sliced banana, peach or
    strawberries

½   cup low-fat milk

2   tablespoons honey

1 Combine the yogurt, fruit, milk and honey in a blender container. Process for 1 to 2 minutes or until smooth.

2 Pour into individual glasses.

SERVES 2

MELON COOLER

3   cups chopped honeydew melon

3   tablespoons sugar

2   tablespoons fresh lime juice

2   sprigs of fresh mint

1 Combine the melon, sugar and lime juice in a blender container. Process until smooth.

2 Pour over ice in a glass. Top with the mint.

SERVES 1

Consider reversible pillows made of two different fabrics: one side for spring/ summer, the other for fall/winter.

CREAM OF BROCCOLI SOUP

2   cups water

1   (16-ounce) package frozen
      broccoli cuts

½   cup chopped onion

½   cup melted butter or margarine

½   cup flour

6   cups milk

4   chicken bouillon cubes

1   teaspoon pepper or white pepper

1 Bring the water to a boil in a medium saucepan. Add the broccoli and reduce the heat. Simmer, covered, for 5 minutes; remove from the heat.

2 Sauté the onion in the butter in a heavy saucepan over low heat for 10 minutes or until tender. Stir in the flour until smooth. Cook for 1 minute, stirring constantly. Stir in the milk gradually and add the bouillon cubes. Cook over medium heat until thickened, stirring constantly.

3 Drain the broccoli and add to the soup. Season with the pepper. Simmer for 20 to 30 minutes or until of the desired consistency, stirring occasionally.

SERVES 6

For a summer tonic, slipcover a sofa or loveseat and chairs in floral or crisp contrasting colors. A lively print in painterly florals or a lemon yellow slipcover with blue contrast cording will not only refresh the room, it will energize it. Even in warm climates where slipcovers are not the norm, the visual change of fabric on upholstered furniture is a tonic for a tired room.

CARROT AND GINGER SOUP

1   large yellow onion, chopped

3   garlic cloves, finely chopped

¼   cup finely chopped fresh gingerroot

6   tablespoons butter

4   (14-ounce) cans chicken broth

1   cup dry white wine

1½   pounds carrots, peeled, chopped

2   tablespoons fresh lemon juice

     curry powder, salt and freshly ground pepper to taste

1   Sauté the onion, garlic and ginger in the butter in a large saucepan over medium heat for 15 to 20 minutes. Add the chicken broth, wine and carrots. Bring to a boil and reduce the heat to medium. Simmer for 45 minutes or until the carrots are very tender.

2   Process the mixture in a blender or food processor. Return to the saucepan and add the lemon juice, curry powder, salt and pepper. Serve hot or chilled; garnish servings with chives or parsley.

SERVES 6

CLAM AND SMOKED SALMON CHOWDER

8   ounces bacon, chopped

1   medium onion, chopped

4   ribs celery, chopped

½   cup chopped green bell pepper

½   cup cooked chopped carrot

2   cups chopped potatoes

1   cup corn kernels

1   pound clams

1   pound smoked salmon fillet, flaked

1   (8-ounce) bottle clam juice

1   bay leaf

2   cups cream

     potato flour

1   tablespoon dillweed

1   Sauté the bacon in a saucepan until crisp. Remove the bacon with a slotted spoon to drain on paper towels; drain the saucepan, reserving 2 tablespoons of the drippings in the saucepan.

2   Add the onion, celery and green pepper to the saucepan and sauté until the onion is translucent. Add the carrot, potatoes, corn, clams, salmon, clam juice, bay leaf and cream. Simmer for 15 minutes or just until the potatoes are tender; do not boil.

3   Blend a small amount of potato flour with enough water to make a thin paste. Stir into the chowder. Simmer just until thickened, stirring constantly. Stir in the bacon and dillweed. Remove bay leaf and serve.

SERVES 4 TO 6

CIOPPINO

6 tablespoons olive oil

4½ cups chopped onions

1½ leeks, trimmed, minced

5 garlic cloves, minced

3 green bell peppers, cut into strips

6 cups canned chopped tomatoes

1 cup fresh or canned tomato sauce

1½ bay leaves

1½ teaspoons oregano

1½ teaspoons thyme

1½ tablespoons basil

¼ teaspoon red pepper flakes

salt and freshly ground black pepper
to taste

2 to 3 cups fish stock or water

1½ cups fresh or bottled clam juice

1½ cups dry white wine

1½ pounds striped bass or other firm fish,
cut into bite-size pieces

18 ounces fresh scallops

1½ pounds shrimp, peeled, deveined

18 small clams in shells, washed

½ pint oysters with juice

1 (12-ounce) lobster tail, cooked in the
shell (optional)

1 hard-shell crab, cooked in the shell,
cracked (optional), or equivalent
amount of crab meat

Cioppino, an Italian fish soup, is a meal in a bowl. Just add a green salad, crusty bread, and a great zinfandel. It has a lot of ingredients, but it comes together quickly.

1 Heat the olive oil in a large saucepan. Add the onions, leeks and garlic and sauté until the vegetables are light brown. Add the green peppers and sauté until wilted. Stir in the tomatoes with their juices, tomato sauce, bay leaves, oregano, thyme, basil, red pepper flakes, salt and black pepper. Add the fish stock.

2 Simmer, covered, for 2 hours, stirring frequently and adding additional fish stock if needed. Add the clam juice and wine. Simmer for 10 minutes longer. The soup may be prepared in advance to this point and returned to a boil to finish.

3 Add the fish to the soup and simmer for 5 minutes. Add the scallops and shrimp. Simmer for 8 minutes. Add the clams, oysters, lobster tail and crab. Cook for 5 minutes or until the clams open, stirring gently; discard the bay leaves. Serve with a side dish of additional red pepper flakes.

SERVES 8

STEAMBOAT CREAM OF CRAB SOUP

½   cup butter

¼   cup flour

1   (14-ounce) can chicken broth

1½ quarts half-and-half

1   pound backfin crab meat

½   cup dry sherry

1   teaspoon salt

¼   teaspoon white pepper

    Old Bay seasoning

1   Melt the butter in a heavy saucepan over low heat. Stir in the flour. Cook for 1 minute or until smooth, stirring constantly. Stir in the chicken broth gradually. Cook over medium heat until thickened and bubbly, stirring constantly.

2   Add the half-and-half, crab meat, sherry, salt and white pepper. Simmer over low heat for 10 to 15 minutes or until heated through, stirring frequently; do not boil. Sprinkle with Old Bay seasoning to serve.

SERVES 8

MONASTERY LENTIL SOUP

2   large onions, chopped

1   carrot, chopped

¼   cup olive oil

½   teaspoon marjoram

½   teaspoon thyme

3   cups beef or chicken stock

1   cup dried lentils

1   (16-ounce) can tomatoes

¼   cup chopped parsley

    salt to taste

½   cup sherry

    shredded Swiss cheese

1   Sauté the onions and carrot in the olive oil in a large saucepan for 3 minutes. Add the marjoram and thyme. Cook for 1 minute longer.

2   Add the beef stock, lentils, tomatoes, parsley and salt. Simmer, covered, until the lentils are tender. Stir in the sherry. Ladle over shredded Swiss cheese to serve.

SERVES 4

CORDON BLEU SOUP

1 chicken, cut up

¼ cup butter

½ cup flour

1 cup half-and-half

2 (14-ounce) cans chicken broth

1 cup chablis or chardonnay

¾ to 1 cup chopped cooked ham

1 bay leaf

garlic salt, salt and pepper to taste

mozzarella cheese

1 Cook the chicken in water to cover in a large saucepan until very tender. Remove the chicken, reserving the cooking liquid. Chop into bite-size pieces, discarding the skin and bones.

2 Melt the butter in a large saucepan. Stir in the flour and cook until bubbly. Remove from the heat and stir in the half-and-half gradually. Cook over low heat until thickened, stirring frequently.

3 Add the reserved cooking liquid, canned chicken broth and wine gradually, stirring constantly. Add the chicken, ham, bay leaf, garlic salt, salt and pepper. Cook until heated through; discard the bay leaf. Sprinkle servings with shredded mozzarella cheese. Serve with French bread and salad.

SERVES 10

Add a dash of color. Take colors from your interior furnishings and pull out the strongest, most colorful hues for accessories with punch: new pillows, placemats and napkins, a tableskirt, a lampshade, an ottoman, a vase or bowl. A dose of undiluted color will add a lively note to your rooms and make all the other colors seem more vibrant.

ITALIAN POTATO SOUP

8	ounces hot Italian sausage, chopped
3	cups chopped peeled potatoes
1	cup chopped onion
1	(15-ounce) can Italian-style tomatoes
1	tablespoon each basil and parsley flakes
1	teaspoon each oregano and salt
1	(15-ounce) can tomato sauce
2	(14-ounce) cans chicken broth
3	cups water

Freeze the sausage to make it easy to cut into small pieces.

1 Sauté the sausage in a 5- to 6-quart saucepan until the fat is rendered; drain. Add the potatoes, onion, chopped tomatoes, basil, parsley, oregano and salt. Stir in the tomato sauce, chicken broth and water.

2 Bring to a boil and reduce the heat. Simmer until the potatoes and onion are tender.

SERVES 4

YELLOW PEPPER SOUP

6	yellow bell peppers, cut lengthwise into halves
3	large onions, chopped
1	cup chopped leeks
½	teaspoon salt
½	teaspoon freshly ground pepper
¼	cup unsalted butter
3	small boiling potatoes, peeled, sliced
5	cups chicken broth
2	tablespoons chopped chives
	toasted croutons
	extra-virgin olive oil
	grated Parmesan cheese

Roasting the peppers brings out their full flavor for this excellent soup.

1 Chop 6 of the pepper halves coarsely and set aside. Place the remaining 6 pepper halves cut side down on a foil-lined baking sheet. Broil in a preheated broiler 2 inches from the heat source for 5 to 10 minutes or until charred. Seal in a plastic bag and steam for 10 minutes. Remove and discard the skins; chop the peppers.

2 Sauté the onions and leeks with the salt and pepper in the butter in a large saucepan over low heat for 10 to 15 minutes or until the onions are translucent. Add the chopped peppers, roasted peppers, potatoes and chicken broth. Bring to a boil and reduce the heat. Simmer for 30 minutes or until the vegetables are tender.

3 Purée the soup in several batches in a food processor. Combine in the saucepan and cook just until heated through. Garnish the servings with chives, croutons, a drizzle of olive oil and cheese.

SERVES 7 OR 8

RIBOLLITA

1   large onion, finely chopped

3   or 4 garlic cloves, minced

4   carrots, peeled, finely chopped

4   ribs celery, finely chopped

1   cup finely chopped fresh parsley

2   teaspoons thyme

6   tablespoons olive oil

2   large potatoes, peeled, cut into
     ½-inch chunks

3   small zucchini, thinly sliced

1   small head green cabbage, shredded

1   (28-ounce) can plum tomatoes

8   ounces Swiss chard or beet greens,
     trimmed

10   ounces fresh or thawed frozen spinach,
     chopped

2½   quarts chicken broth

2   cups dry red wine

1   cup canned cannellini beans or white
     kidney beans

     salt and freshly ground pepper
     to taste

8   (1-inch) slices dried Italian or French
     bread

1½ cups grated Parmesan cheese

½   cup extra-virgin olive oil

4   scallions, trimmed, minced

½   cup grated Parmesan cheese

Ribollita is a thick Tuscan soup. Somewhat like minestrone, it is best made a day in advance, then ladled over slices of dried bread and Parmesan cheese. When it is reheated (the name means reboiled), the bread falls apart, making a hearty soup—a meal in a bowl!

1   Sauté the onion, garlic, carrots, celery, parsley and thyme in 6 tablespoons heated olive oil in a large stockpot for 15 minutes, stirring frequently.

2   Add the potatoes, zucchini, cabbage, undrained tomatoes, Swiss chard and spinach and toss to mix well. Stir in the chicken broth and red wine. Simmer for 1 to 1¼ hours or until the vegetables are tender. Add the cannellini beans and season with salt and pepper. Cook for 15 minutes.

3   Ladle ⅓ of the soup into a stockpot. Top with 4 slices of the bread and ¾ cup cheese. Add ½ of the remaining soup and top with the remaining bread and ¾ cup cheese. Ladle the remaining soup over the top. Chill, covered, for 8 hours or longer.

4   Reheat the soup over medium heat for about 30 minutes or until heated through, stirring frequently. Garnish servings with a drizzle of extra-virgin olive oil, scallions and a sprinkle of the ½ cup cheese.

SERVES 10 TO 12

TUSCAN TOMATO BREAD SOUP

2 (16-ounce) cans tomatoes, drained

2 cups (1-inch) dried Italian bread cubes

vegetable broth or cold water

1 onion, finely chopped

3 tablespoons extra-virgin olive oil

3 or 4 garlic cloves, finely chopped, or to taste

1½ to 2 cups tomato juice, or to taste

3 tablespoons minced basil

1 tablespoon balsamic vinegar

salt and freshly ground pepper to taste

fresh basil leaves

3 tablespoons extra-virgin olive oil

Substitute fresh tomatoes and take advantage of the basil in your summer garden for this simple soup. It is just as good with low-salt tomatoes and tomato juice.

1 Pulse the tomatoes in a food processor until chopped but not puréed. Soak the bread cubes in the vegetable broth in a bowl until softened. Drain the bread, squeeze dry and chop coarsely.

2 Sauté the onion in 3 tablespoons olive oil in a large saucepan over medium heat for 3 minutes or until tender. Add the garlic and sauté for 1 minute. Stir in the tomatoes, tomato juice and minced basil. Simmer for 10 minutes, stirring occasionally. Add the bread, vinegar, salt and pepper; mix well.

3 Serve at room temperature. Garnish servings with basil leaves and drizzle with 3 tablespoons olive oil.

SERVES 6 TO 8

TOMATO AND LEEK BISQUE

4   leeks

2   ribs celery, coarsely chopped

1   garlic clove, chopped

¼   cup olive oil

1   (28-ounce) can whole peeled tomatoes

1   (14-ounce) can chicken broth

¾   cup dry white wine

1   tablespoon lemon juice

1½   tablespoons chopped fresh basil

½   teaspoon salt

¼   teaspoon white pepper

¾   cup whipping cream

    basil leaves

Even children like this soup that "tastes like pizza." Omit the cream for a lighter version.

1   Chop enough of the white and pale green portions of the leeks to measure 8 cups. Sauté the leeks with the celery and garlic in the olive oil in a large saucepan until the leeks are translucent. Add the tomatoes and chicken broth. Simmer for 30 minutes.

2   Add the wine, lemon juice, basil, salt and white pepper. Simmer for 30 minutes longer. Stir in the cream and simmer just until heated through; do not boil. Garnish servings with basil leaves.

SERVES 6

You can use a king-size comforter on a queen-size bed by rotating it 90 degrees. This will provide a small pillow tuck and more length, with no gap at the top of the bed.

CREAM OF CANTALOUPE SOUP

1   large cantaloupe

2   tablespoons dry vermouth

2   tablespoons brandy

     juice and grated peel of 1 lime

⅓   cup whipping cream

¼   cup sugar, or to taste

¼   teaspoon cinnamon

¼   teaspoon nutmeg

     lime peel curls

Great served in bowls for summer garden parties or showers, or served in wine glasses for a buffet.

1   Peel and seed the cantaloupe and cut into chunks. Process in a food processor until coarsely chopped but not puréed.

2   Combine with the vermouth, brandy, lime juice and lime peel in a bowl and whisk until well mixed. Add the cream, sugar, cinnamon and nutmeg and mix well. Chill until serving time. Garnish servings with lime curls.

SERVES 6

GAZPACHO

1   (32-ounce) can stewed tomatoes

1½   cups chopped celery

2   green bell peppers, chopped

6   to 8 green onions, chopped

2   avocados, finely chopped

½   (12-ounce) bottle chili sauce

      Tabasco sauce to taste

3   tablespoons balsamic vinegar

Ideal for picnics on the beach or as a refreshing first course on a hot day.

1   Combine the tomatoes, celery, green peppers, green onions and avocados in a bowl. Add the chili sauce, Tabasco sauce and vinegar and mix gently.

2   Chill, covered, for 4 hours or longer.

SERVES 4

CHILLED SHRIMP AND CUCUMBER SOUP

2   large cucumbers, peeled, coarsely chopped

¼   cup red wine vinegar

1   tablespoon sugar

1   teaspoon salt

1   pound small shrimp, peeled, deveined

2   tablespoons unsalted butter

¼   cup dry vermouth

     salt and pepper to taste

1½   cups chilled buttermilk

¾   cup (or more) chopped fresh dill

     dill sprigs

A refreshing, tasty way to begin a summer dinner party.

1   Toss the cucumbers with the vinegar, sugar and 1 teaspoon salt in a bowl. Let stand for 30 minutes.

2   Rinse the shrimp and pat dry. Sauté in the butter in a small skillet for 2 to 3 minutes or until pink. Remove to a bowl with a slotted spoon.

3   Add the vermouth to the skillet. Cook until reduced to several spoonfuls. Pour over the shrimp in the bowl and season with salt and pepper to taste.

4   Drain the cucumbers and place in a food processor container. Pulse several times. Add the buttermilk and process until smooth. Add ¾ cup dill and process for 1 second. Add to the shrimp.

5   Chill in the refrigerator. Serve in chilled bowls. Garnish with dill sprigs.

SERVES 4 TO 6

Make a lace tablecloth for an oval or rectangular table by buying 2⅜ yards of lace 60 inches wide. Sew a simple hem at both ends and you'll have a tableskirt 60 by 84 inches when finished. Place the lace over a pretty colored basecloth that is the same size, and vary the color of the base-cloth with the season.

BLUEBERRY CREAM SALAD

1   (3-ounce) package lemon gelatin

1   (3-ounce) package black raspberry or grape gelatin

1   cup boiling water

½   cup cold water

1   tablespoon lemon juice

1   (21-ounce) can blueberry pie filling

¼   cup confectioners' sugar

1   cup sour cream

Garnish with a fresh flower, a mint sprig, or a sprig of artificial holly, depending on the season.

1 Mix the lemon gelatin and raspberry gelatin in a bowl. Add the boiling water and stir until the gelatins dissolve. Add the cold water and lemon juice. Stir in the pie filling. Spoon into a 1-quart dish. Chill until firm.

2 Blend the confectioners' sugar and sour cream in a small bowl. Spread over the salad. Cut into squares to serve.

SERVES 12

PRETZEL SALAD

2   cups crushed pretzels

¾   cup melted margarine or butter

8   ounces cream cheese, softened

1   cup sugar

8   ounces whipped topping

1   (6-ounce) package orange gelatin

2   cups boiling water

1   (16-ounce) can crushed pineapple

1   (8-ounce) can mandarin oranges, drained

A wonderful summertime salad. You may want to serve it for a light dessert!

1 Mix the crushed pretzels and margarine in a bowl. Press into a 9x13-inch dish. Bake at 400 degrees for 8 minutes. Cool completely.

2 Combine the cream cheese, sugar and whipped topping in a bowl and blend until smooth. Spread over the pretzel layer, sealing to the edge of the dish.

3 Dissolve the gelatin in the boiling water in a bowl. Add the pineapple and oranges and mix well. Let stand until cool. Spread over the cream cheese layer.

4 Chill until firm. Cut into squares to serve.

SERVES 12

SUPPER SALAD MOLD

1   (3-ounce) package lemon gelatin

1   cup boiling water

1   tablespoon grated onion

½   teaspoon salt

½   cup whipping cream, whipped

½   cup mayonnaise

8   ounces shredded cooked crab meat
     or shrimp

8   ounces mild Cheddar cheese, cubed

3   hard-cooked eggs, chopped

2   tablespoons chopped green bell
     pepper

2   cups chopped celery

½   cup broken walnuts

1   Dissolve the gelatin in the boiling water in a bowl. Stir in the onion and salt. Chill just until of the consistency of egg white. Fold in the whipped cream and mayonnaise.

2   Add the crab meat, cheese, eggs, green pepper, celery and walnuts and mix gently. Spoon into a fish-shape mold. Chill until firm. Unmold onto a serving plate.

SERVES 4

SUMMER CHICKEN SALAD

2   cups frozen peas

2   chicken breast halves, cooked,
     chilled, chopped

     juice of 1 lemon

1   red bell pepper, chopped

2   cups cooked brown rice

1   tablespoon minced fresh tarragon,
     or ½ tablespoon dried leaves

10   peppercorns, coarsely crushed

⅓   cup mayonnaise

⅓   cup fat-free plain yogurt

1   Rinse the peas under cold water in a colander, shaking several times; drain well. Toss the chicken with the lemon juice in a bowl. Add the peas, bell pepper, rice, tarragon and peppercorns and mix gently.

2   Blend the mayonnaise and yogurt in a small bowl. Add to the chicken mixture and stir lightly to mix. Chill until serving time.

SERVES 5

CURRIED CHICKEN SALAD

4	large chicken breasts
1	cup water
2	chicken bouillon cubes
2	ribs celery, sliced
1	medium onion, chopped
1	cup uncooked white rice, or 1/2 cup white rice and 1/2 cup wild rice
2	cups chicken broth
2	cups chopped celery
1	green bell pepper, or 1/2 green bell pepper and 1/2 red bell pepper, chopped
1	large onion, chopped
5	green onions with tops, chopped
1	cup seedless green grape halves
2	tablespoons (or more) curry powder
2	cups mayonnaise
1	head lettuce, chopped, shredded

1 Combine the chicken with the water, bouillon cubes, 2 ribs sliced celery and medium onion in a saucepan. Simmer for 20 to 30 minutes or until the chicken is tender. Cool in the cooking liquid and chill in the refrigerator. Cook the rice in the chicken broth in a saucepan using the package directions. Chill the rice in the refrigerator.

2 Remove the chicken from the cooking liquid and chop into bite-size pieces. Combine with 2 cups celery, bell pepper, 1 chopped onion, green onions and grapes in a large bowl and mix gently.

3 Heat the curry powder in a sauté pan over medium heat for 1 minute or until the fragrance is released, stirring constantly; do not burn. Remove from the heat and stir in the mayonnaise. Add to the chicken mixture and mix lightly.

4 Layer the shredded lettuce in a 3- to 4-quart serving dish or large platter. Layer the rice and chicken mixture over the lettuce. Chill for 4 hours or longer.

5 Serve with condiments such as toasted coconut tossed with 1 teaspoon confectioners' sugar and 1 cup raisins; toasted almonds; peanuts; chutney; or additional grapes and peppers.

SERVES 8

CHÈVRE AND ARUGULA SALAD

8 cups arugula leaves

6 ounces Montrachet or other soft mild chèvre cheese, crumbled

¼ cup balsamic vinegar

½ cup Trastevere Dressing

The dressing for this salad is also delicious with other greens.

1 Place the arugula leaves on salad plates. Sprinkle with the cheese and drizzle with the vinegar.

2 Spoon a dollop of the Trastevere Dressing over each of the salads. Serve immediately.

SERVES 6

Trastevere Dressing

8 medium tomatoes, seeded, chopped

1 small yellow onion, cut into slivers lengthwise

3 garlic cloves, minced

2 cups extra-virgin olive oil

salt and freshly ground pepper to taste

2 tablespoons fresh lemon juice

1 teaspoon sugar

Bring this dressing to a simmer if you don't have time to let it stand for several hours to blend the flavors.

1 Combine the tomatoes with the onion and garlic in a medium saucepan. Stir in the oil and season with salt and pepper. Stir in the lemon juice and sugar.

2 Let stand over a pilot light or in another warm place for several hours to blend the flavors.

MAKES 4 CUPS

After a family gathering including children, bring out a white duck tablecloth and ask them to make a "memory cloth" by drawing pictures with their names, and date them. Crayons will work, but permanent felt-tip markers will last through a cleaning after the next family celebration.

BOK CHOY SALAD

2　packages ramen noodles

1　(2-ounce) package slivered almonds

⅓　cup sesame seeds

½　cup butter

1　large head bok choy, shredded

5　scallions, chopped

1　cup sugar

1　cup sesame oil

¼　cup red wine vinegar or balsamic
　　vinegar

3　tablespoons soy sauce

Add chopped cooked chicken or canned chicken for a main dish salad.

1　Crush the ramen noodles in the packages; reserve the seasoning packets from the noodles for another use. Toast the noodles, almonds and sesame seeds in the butter in a skillet. Cool to room temperature. Combine with the bok choy and scallions in a serving bowl. Chill, covered, in the refrigerator.

2　Mix the sugar, sesame oil, vinegar and soy sauce in a small bowl. Add to the salad 20 minutes before serving and mix gently.

SERVES 8

BROCCOLI AND CRANBERRY SLAW

2　cups broccoli florets

1¼　cups fresh or dried cranberries

4　cups shredded cabbage

1　small onion, minced

8　slices crisp-fried bacon, crumbled

1　cup raisins

1　cup coarsely chopped walnuts

⅓　cup sugar

2　tablespoons cider vinegar

1　cup mayonnaise

1　Combine the broccoli, cranberries, cabbage, onion, bacon, raisins and walnuts in a bowl and mix well.

2　Blend the sugar, vinegar and mayonnaise in a small bowl. Add to the salad and toss gently. Chill for 20 minutes.

SERVES 8

NAPA CABBAGE SLAW

½ cup slivered almonds

6 cups shredded Napa cabbage

1 cup thinly sliced radishes

1 cup thinly sliced green onions

1 cup slivered pea pods

1 cup chopped fresh cilantro

Napa Dressing

Add red cabbage for color and variety. Chop the vegetables by hand rather than in a food processor.

1 Sprinkle the almonds on a baking sheet. Toast at 350 degrees for 10 minutes or until light brown.

2 Combine the cabbage, radishes, green onions, pea pods and cilantro in a serving bowl and mix well. Chill for 8 hours or longer. Add the Napa Dressing and toasted almonds and toss gently.

SERVES 8 TO 10

Napa Dressing

3 tablespoons white wine vinegar

1 tablespoon soy sauce

3 tablespoons sugar

1 garlic clove, minced

1 cup mayonnaise

¼ teaspoon sesame oil

½ teaspoon ground ginger

¼ teaspoon cayenne pepper

1 Combine the vinegar, soy sauce, sugar, garlic, mayonnaise, sesame oil, ginger and cayenne pepper in a bowl and mix well.

2 Store in the refrigerator until needed.

MAKES 1¼ CUPS

Make a king-size sham for a twin bed—it's the perfect size to fill out the entire 39-inch bed.

PACIFIC RIM CAESAR SALAD

1   garlic clove, finely minced

¼   cup unsalted butter

1   cup dried bread cubes

2   heads Romaine lettuce

½   cup extra-virgin olive oil

3   or 4 tablespoons lemon juice

     Worcestershire sauce to taste

     salt and pepper to taste

1   egg

2   slices crisp-fried bacon, chopped

¼   cup crushed unsalted roasted peanuts

2   teaspoons grated lime peel

1   red bell pepper, finely chopped

½   cup grated Parmesan cheese

1   Sauté the garlic in the butter in a 12-inch skillet over medium-high heat until sizzling. Add the bread cubes and sauté for 8 minutes or until brown. Remove the bread cubes with a slotted spoon, discarding the garlic; set aside.

2   Separate and wash the lettuce, reserving the outer leaves for another use. Arrange the inner leaves in the same direction in a large bowl. Drizzle with half the olive oil and 3 tablespoons of the lemon juice and toss gently. Add the Worcestershire sauce, salt and pepper; toss gently. Drizzle with the remaining olive oil.

3   Place the egg in rapidly boiling water to cover and cook for exactly 30 seconds. Chill quickly under cold water and break into a bowl. Beat lightly with a fork and pour over the lettuce; toss gently.

4   Sprinkle with the bacon, croutons, peanuts, lime peel, bell pepper and half the cheese; mix evenly. Adjust the seasonings and lemon juice. Spoon onto serving plates and sprinkle with the remaining cheese.

SERVES 4 TO 6

SUPER SPINACH SALAD

1   (11-ounce) can mandarin oranges

1   (8-ounce) can water chestnuts

     fresh spinach leaves, torn

     fresh or canned bean sprouts

¼   cup chopped green onions

¼   cup chopped walnuts

½   cup Russian salad dressing

1   (12-ounce) can Chinese noodles

1   Drain the mandarin oranges and water chestnuts.

2   Combine with the spinach, bean sprouts, green onions and walnuts in a large bowl and mix lightly.

3   Add the salad dressing and toss to coat well. Top with the noodles at serving time.

4   Substitute sweet-and-sour or poppy seed dressing for the Russian salad dressing if preferred.

SERVES 8

GERMAN POTATO SALAD

6	medium potatoes
6	slices bacon
¾	cup chopped onion
2	tablespoons flour
¼	cup (or more) sugar
½	teaspoon celery seeds
1½	teaspoons salt
	pepper to taste
¾	cup water
⅓	cup vinegar

1 Boil the unpeeled potatoes in water to cover in a large saucepan until tender; drain and cool. Peel the potatoes and cut into thin slices.

2 Fry the bacon in a skillet until crisp; remove and drain on paper towels, reserving the drippings in the skillet; crumble the bacon. Add the onion to the skillet and sauté until golden brown. Stir in the flour, sugar, celery seeds, salt and pepper. Remove from the heat.

3 Stir in ¾ cup water and vinegar. Bring to a boil and cook for 1 minute or until thickened, stirring constantly. Add the potato slices and crumbled bacon and mix gently. Remove from the heat and let stand, covered, until serving time; serve warm.

SERVES 8

For spring and summer, take stock of your exterior views and rearrange the furniture to take advantage of the garden and the great outdoors. Pull furniture away from the walls. Reorient the major seating pieces away from the fireplace and toward the best views. Place a favorite chair where you can watch the birds while you read.

MANDARIN TOSSED SALAD

½ to 1 head lettuce, shredded, or torn spinach

1 cup sliced celery

2 green onions with tops, sliced

1 tablespoon minced parsley

1 (11-ounce) can mandarin oranges, drained, patted dry

½ cup toasted slivered almonds

Spicy Vinaigrette

1 Combine the lettuce, celery, green onions and parsley in a salad bowl. Add the mandarin oranges and almonds. Toss to mix well.

2 Drizzle with the Spicy Vinaigrette and toss to coat well.

SERVES 4

Spicy Vinaigrette

¼ cup vegetable oil

2 tablespoons tarragon vinegar

2 tablespoons sugar

½ teaspoon Tabasco sauce

½ teaspoon salt

freshly ground pepper to taste

1 Combine the oil, vinegar, sugar, Tabasco sauce, salt and pepper in a jar and mix well.

2 Chill until serving time. Shake well before using.

MAKES ½ CUP

RICE SALAD WITH ARTICHOKES

1   (6-ounce) jar marinated artichoke
     hearts
2   (7-ounce) packages chicken-flavor
     Rice-A-Roni
½   green bell pepper, chopped
4   green onions, chopped
½   cup chopped green olives
½   cup mayonnaise
1   teaspoon curry powder

1   Drain and chop the artichokes, reserving the liquid. Cook the Rice-A-Roni using the package directions and cool to room temperature. Combine with the artichokes, green pepper, green onions and olives in a bowl and mix well.

2   Blend the reserved artichoke liquid with the mayonnaise and curry powder in a small bowl. Add to the salad and toss to coat well. Chill, covered, for 8 hours or longer.

SERVES 6 TO 8

PICNIC RICE SALAD

4   cups cooked brown rice
2   large tomatoes, or 8 cherry tomatoes,
     chopped
6   scallions, thinly sliced
1   (2.5-ounce) can sliced black olives,
     drained
¼   cup shredded fresh basil leaves
⅓   cup salted sunflower seed kernels
¼   cup olive oil
1½   tablespoons balsamic vinegar
     salt and pepper to taste

1   Combine the rice, tomatoes, scallions, olives, basil and sunflower seed kernels in a bowl and mix well.

2   Whisk the olive oil, vinegar, salt and pepper in a small bowl. Add to the rice mixture and toss to coat well. Chill, covered, for 3 hours.

SERVES 6

MEATS · POULTRY · SEAFOOD

BARBECUED BRISKET

½ (3-ounce) bottle liquid smoke

2 teaspoons onion salt

2 teaspoons celery salt

1 teaspoon garlic powder

1 (5-pound) beef brisket

4 to 5 teaspoons Worcestershire sauce

½ cup barbecue sauce

1 Mix the liquid smoke, onion salt, celery salt and garlic powder in a bowl. Rub the mixture over the surface of the brisket. Wrap the brisket in heavy foil. Let stand in the refrigerator for 8 to 10 hours.

2 Open the foil and drizzle the Worcestershire sauce over the brisket; reseal the foil. Bake at 300 degrees for 4 hours. Open the foil and pour the barbecue sauce over the brisket; reseal the foil.

3 Bake at 350 degrees for 1 hour longer. Serve hot or at room temperature. Add additional barbecue sauce and serve on hamburger buns.

SERVES 10 TO 12

Custom placemats may be rectangular or oval, quilted or unquilted, lined or unlined. Lined placemats may be "pillowcase lined" (to the edge) or banded with bias fabric. Cording or ruffling may also be added. One-half yard of fabric makes two placemats, unlined and unquilted, or one self-lined placemat.

DAMN GOOD STEW

2   pounds lean beef chuck, cubed

2   (16-ounce) cans tomatoes

½   small onion, sliced

1   cup chopped celery

6   carrots, chopped

3   potatoes, chopped

1   (15-ounce) can tomato sauce

½   to 1 cup burgundy

3   tablespoons quick-cooking tapioca

1   tablespoon sugar

    salt and pepper to taste

    mushrooms

Add a small amount of sherry for extra flavor.

1   Combine the beef chuck, undrained tomatoes, onion, celery, carrots, potatoes, tomato sauce, wine, tapioca, sugar, salt and pepper in a baking dish. Bake at 250 degrees for 5 to 5½ hours.

2   Stir in the mushrooms. Bake for 20 to 30 minutes longer.

SERVES 6

SPICY NEW ENGLAND POT ROAST

1   (4-pound) bottom round beef pot roast

3   tablespoons flour

2   teaspoons salt

¼   teaspoon pepper

3   tablespoons vegetable oil

1   bunch carrots, peeled

16   small white onions

1   cup whole or jellied cranberry sauce

1   cup beef broth

½   cup grated horseradish

1   cinnamon stick, broken into halves

4   whole cloves

Don't be put off by the amount of horseradish. It loses its pungency as it cooks.

1   Coat the pot roast on all sides with a mixture of the flour, salt and pepper. Heat the oil in a Dutch oven over high heat until hot. Add the pot roast. Brown on all sides, turning frequently.

2   Cut the carrots into 3-inch pieces. Add the carrots, onions, cranberry sauce, broth, horseradish, cinnamon stick and cloves to the Dutch oven and mix well. Bring to a boil.

3   Bake, covered, at 300 degrees for 3 to 4 hours or until the roast is done to taste. Serve with mashed potatoes.

SERVES 8

PEPPER STEAK

2 beef bouillon cubes

1 cup hot water

2 tablespoons cornstarch

2 tablespoons soy sauce

½ teaspoon garlic salt

⅛ teaspoon pepper

1½ pounds beef round steak, cut into
½-inch cubes

¼ cup vegetable oil

⅛ teaspoon ginger

8 ounces green bell peppers, sliced

8 ounces fresh mushrooms, sliced

8 ounces fresh tomatoes, sliced

hot cooked rice

1 Dissolve the bouillon cubes in the hot water and mix well. Mix the cornstarch, soy sauce, garlic salt and pepper in a bowl. Add the beef, stirring until coated.

2 Heat the oil in a skillet, or to 350 degrees in an electric skillet. Add the ginger and beef mixture. Sauté for 2 minutes. Add the green peppers and mushrooms and mix well. Stir in the bouillon.

3 Cook, covered, until thickened, stirring occasionally. Add the tomatoes just before serving. Cook, covered, for several minutes. Serve over the rice.

SERVES 4 TO 6

If your windows are too small for the room, try these ideas: extend rods beyond the window frame so that maximum light comes into the room when the draperies are open; create the illusion of height by adding a valance or shade over the window so that the bottom edge just covers the top of the frame; place tiebacks lower on the window to make it seem wider.

JAMAICAN STUFFED PUMPKIN

1 (8- to 10-inch) pumpkin or Hubbard
  squash

  salt to taste

2 tablespoons vegetable oil

2 pounds ground beef

8 ounces ground smoked ham

2½ cups finely chopped onions

1 green or red bell pepper, finely
  chopped

2¼ teaspoons salt

2 teaspoons olive oil

2 teaspoons oregano

1 teaspoon vinegar

1 teaspoon ground black pepper

1 teaspoon shredded gingerroot

2 large garlic cloves, crushed

⅛ teaspoon crushed dried red pepper

1 (8-ounce) can tomato sauce

½ cup raisins

⅓ cup sliced pimento-stuffed green
  olives

2 teaspoons minced drained capers

3 eggs, beaten

1 Cut a 5-inch circle from the top of the pumpkin and reserve. Scrape the inside clean, discarding the seeds and membranes. Place the pumpkin in a large stockpot and add enough salted water to cover. Cover and bring to a boil; reduce the heat. Simmer for 25 minutes or until the pumpkin is almost tender. Drain and pat dry. Sprinkle the inside of the pumpkin lightly with salt.

2 Heat the vegetable oil in a skillet. Add the ground beef, ground ham, onions and green pepper. Cook over high heat until the ground beef is brown and crumbly, stirring constantly; drain. Mix 2¼ teaspoons salt, olive oil, oregano, vinegar, black pepper, gingerroot, garlic and red pepper in a bowl. Stir into the ground beef mixture. Add the tomato sauce, raisins, green olives and capers and mix well.

3 Cook, covered, over low heat for 15 minutes, stirring occasionally. Remove from the heat and cool slightly. Stir in the eggs. Spoon into the pumpkin and pat firmly. Top with the reserved pumpkin lid.

4 Place in a greased shallow baking pan. Bake at 350 degrees for 1 hour. Remove from the oven. Let stand for 10 to 15 minutes. Remove to a large serving platter and garnish as desired. Spoon out portions of pumpkin and stuffing to serve, keeping skin intact.

SERVES 6 TO 8

SIRLOIN STEAKS WITH BLEU CHEESE BUTTER

- 6 ounces bleu cheese, crumbled
- ¼ cup butter, softened
- 2 tablespoons chopped fresh Italian parsley
- ¾ teaspoon rosemary, crushed
- ¼ cup chopped walnuts, toasted
- salt and pepper to taste
- 1 tablespoon rosemary, crushed
- 6 large garlic cloves
- 1½ teaspoons salt
- 1½ teaspoons ground pepper
- 2 (1½- to 1¾-pound) top sirloin or strip steaks, 1 inch thick

1 Combine the bleu cheese, butter, parsley and ¾ teaspoon rosemary in a bowl and mix well. Stir in the walnuts. Season with salt and pepper to taste. Store, covered, in the refrigerator for up to 2 days. Bring to room temperature before serving.

2 Combine 1 tablespoon rosemary, garlic, 1½ teaspoons salt and 1½ teaspoons pepper in a food processor container. Process until the mixture resembles a coarse paste.

3 Pat the steaks dry. Rub 2 teaspoons of the garlic paste on each side of the steaks. Arrange in a large dish. Let stand, covered, at room temperature for 1 hour.

4 Grill over medium-high heat for 5 minutes per side for medium-rare or until done to taste, turning once or twice. Transfer the steaks to a serving platter. Let stand for 5 minutes.

5 Cut each steak into 3 equal portions. Top each portion with some of the bleu cheese walnut butter. Serve immediately.

SERVES 6

A silver or gold lamé tablecloth will add a million dollars' worth of "glam" to a holiday party. Or take lengths of lamé and tie them tightly around chair backs, making large bows. Trim the ends at an angle with sharp scissors.

ITALIAN MEAT LOAF

2   **pounds ground beef**

1   **pound sweet Italian sausage, crumbled**

3   **cups bread crumbs**

1   **cup chopped fresh parsley**

1   **onion, chopped**

5   **garlic cloves, minced**

2   **tablespoons basil**

    salt and pepper to taste

4   **eggs, lightly beaten**

½   **cup tomato juice**

½   **cup dry red wine**

4   **ounces sun-dried tomatoes, softened, drained**

1   **pound smoked mozzarella cheese, cut into strips**

1   Mix the ground beef, sausage, bread crumbs, parsley, onion, garlic, basil, salt and pepper in a bowl. Add the eggs, tomato juice and wine and mix well. Pat into a 12x15-inch rectangle on a sheet of waxed paper.

2   Layer the sun-dried tomatoes and half the cheese over the rectangle. Roll as for a jelly roll, peeling back the waxed paper as you roll. Arrange seam side down on a baking sheet lined with foil.

3   Bake at 400 degrees for 1 hour. Top with the remaining cheese. Bake for 10 minutes longer or until the cheese melts. Serve hot with fresh tomato sauce or chilled.

SERVES 6 TO 8

GROUND BEEF STROGANOFF

1 (12- to 16-ounce) package fine
  noodles

  beef broth

2 pounds ground beef

½ cup butter (optional)

2 (6-ounce) cans mushrooms, drained

1 cup chopped onion

1 garlic clove, minced

¼ cup flour

1 cup beef bouillon

⅓ cup chili sauce

2 teaspoons salt

1 teaspoon Worcestershire sauce

½ teaspoon pepper

1½ cups sour cream

1   Cook the noodles al dente in beef broth in a saucepan; drain.

2   Brown the ground beef in ¼ cup of the butter in a skillet, stirring until crumbly; drain. Stir in the remaining ¼ cup butter, mushrooms, onion and garlic.

3   Cook until the onion is brown and tender, stirring constantly. Add the flour and stir until mixed. Stir in the beef bouillon, chili sauce, salt, Worcestershire sauce and pepper. Add the sour cream and mix gently.

4   Layer the noodles and ground beef mixture in a buttered baking dish. Bake at 350 degrees for 1 hour. This may be prepared in advance, adding the sour cream to the ground beef mixture just before baking.

SERVES 6 TO 8

Tiebacks on draperies look best if placed either ⅓ down or ⅔ down from the top, so that a long graceful fall of fabric comes out of—or into—the tieback. If placed in the middle, tiebacks will cut that fall of fabric in half.

SKILLET DINNER MEXICANA

1 pound ground beef

1 (16-ounce) can diced tomatoes

1 (6-ounce) can tomato paste

1 (4-ounce) can chopped green
   chiles, drained

¾ cup chopped onion

¼ cup water

1½ teaspoons chili powder

½ teaspoon garlic salt

½ teaspoon salt

¼ teaspoon pepper

   Cornmeal Dumplings

1 Brown the ground beef in a 12-inch skillet, stirring until crumbly; drain. Stir in the undrained tomatoes, tomato paste, chiles, onion, water, chili powder, garlic salt, salt and pepper. Simmer, covered, for 5 minutes, stirring occasionally.

2 Drop the Cornmeal Dumplings batter by rounded tablespoons onto the hot ground beef mixture. Simmer, uncovered, for 10 minutes. Cover and simmer for 10 minutes longer.

SERVES 6 TO 8

Cornmeal Dumplings

¾ cup flour

½ cup cornmeal

1 tablespoon baking powder

½ teaspoon salt

¼ cup vegetable shortening

1 cup shredded sharp Cheddar cheese

⅔ cup milk

1 Combine the flour, cornmeal, baking powder and salt in a bowl and mix well. Cut in the shortening until crumbly.

2 Stir in the cheese. Add the milk, stirring just until moistened.

SERVES 6 TO 8

TAMALE PIE

1 (12-ounce) can evaporated milk

1¼ cups yellow cornmeal

1 cup water

½ teaspoon salt

1 pound ground beef

1 cup chopped onion

¼ cup chopped green bell pepper

1 garlic clove, minced

1 (16-ounce) can chili beans
without meat

1 (10-ounce) can corn niblets, drained

1 (8-ounce) can tomato sauce

1 (2-ounce) can sliced black olives,
drained

1 tablespoon chili powder

1 teaspoon salt

¼ teaspoon pepper

½ cup shredded Cheddar cheese

Doubling the recipe gives you an extra "frozen dinner" for unexpected company or to serve on those nights you are just too tired to cook.

1 Combine the evaporated milk, cornmeal, water and ½ teaspoon salt in a saucepan and mix well. Cook over medium heat for 5 to 7 minutes or until thickened, stirring frequently. Reserve ½ cup or more of the mixture for the topping. Spread the remaining cornmeal mixture over the bottom and sides of a greased 8x8-inch baking dish. Bake at 425 degrees for 10 minutes.

2 Brown the ground beef with the onion, green pepper and garlic in a skillet, stirring until the ground beef is crumbly; drain. Stir in the chili beans, corn, tomato sauce, black olives, chili powder, 1 teaspoon salt and pepper. Spoon into the prepared baking dish.

3 Drop the reserved cornmeal mixture by rounded spoonfuls over the ground beef mixture. Sprinkle with the cheese. Bake for 15 minutes.

SERVES 6 TO 8

To freshen your dry-clean-only fabric treatments and bed ensembles between cleanings, remove any hooks or pins and place the materials in the dryer on the fluff or air-only cycle with a sheet of fabric softener and a dry terry cloth towel. The towel will absorb any dust or dirt as it is released. Rehang window treatments immediately at the end of the drying cycle.

LAMB CHOPS WITH CANNELLINI AND SPINACH

4   to 6 (1- to 2-inch) lamb chops

     anchovy paste (optional)

1   cup minced shallots

½   cup olive oil

5   large garlic cloves, minced

1   tablespoon chopped fresh rosemary,
     or 1 teaspoon dried rosemary

     salt and pepper to taste

2   (15-ounce) cans cannellini beans

4   plum tomatoes, chopped

2   (10-ounce) packages fresh spinach

1   tablespoon olive oil

1 Rub both sides of the lamb chops with anchovy paste. Mix the shallots, ½ cup olive oil, garlic, rosemary, salt and pepper in a bowl. Pat some of the mixture onto both sides of the lamb chops. Arrange in a single layer in a dish. Chill, covered, for 2 hours or longer.

2 Combine the remaining shallot mixture with the drained beans and tomatoes in a saucepan. Bring to a simmer, stirring to mix well. Season with salt and pepper and keep warm.

3 Grill the lamb chops for 5 minutes on each side for medium-rare, or until done to taste. Spoon the bean mixture onto serving plates; place the chops on the beans.

4 Sauté the spinach in 1 tablespoon olive oil in a skillet just until wilted. Season with salt and pepper to taste. Spoon over the lamb.

SERVES 4 TO 6

UNSTUFFED CABBAGE

1   pound ground lamb, beef, or turkey

½   cup uncooked rice

1   teaspoon Worcestershire sauce

     salt and pepper to taste

2   pounds green cabbage, chopped

1   (28-ounce) can peeled tomatoes

1   (8-ounce) can tomato sauce

1   cup chopped onion

1   cup water

¼   cup honey

¼   cup lemon juice

⅓   cup raisins

1 Combine the ground lamb, rice, Worcestershire sauce, salt and pepper in a bowl and mix well. Shape into 1¼-inch balls with damp hands.

2 Combine the cabbage, undrained tomatoes, tomato sauce, onion, water, honey and lemon juice in a stockpot. Bring to a boil over medium-high heat. Add the meatballs. Reduce heat to medium-low.

3 Simmer, covered, for 2 hours, stirring occasionally. Stir in the raisins. Cook, uncovered, for 30 minutes longer, stirring occasionally.

SERVES 6 TO 8

CHALUPAS

1 pound dried pinto beans

1 (3-pound) pork loin roast

7 cups water

1/2 cup chopped onion

1 (4-ounce) can chopped green chiles

2 garlic cloves, crushed

2 tablespoons chili powder

1 tablespoon cumin

1 tablespoon salt

1 teaspoon oregano

1 Soak the beans in water to cover for 4 to 10 hours; drain.

2 Brown the roast in a Dutch oven at 450 degrees for 20 minutes. Add the beans, 7 cups water, onion, chiles, garlic, chili powder, cumin, salt and oregano and mix well.

3 Bake, covered, at 300 to 325 degrees for 5 hours or until the roast is very tender. Shred the roast with a fork and mix with the beans. Cook until the moisture has been absorbed and the mixture is of the desired consistency, stirring occasionally.

4 Serve with flour tortillas, tortilla chips or corn chips, chopped tomato, chopped cilantro, chopped green onions, chopped avocado, shredded lettuce, salsa, sliced black olives, shredded cheese and/or sour cream.

SERVES 8

For custom napkins, 1/2 yard of 54-inch-wide fabric will make 3 napkins up to 16 inches wide; 5/8 yard will make 2 napkins up to 20 inches wide.

ROASTED HONEY PEPPER PORK

1   (12-ounce) package frozen whole cranberries, coarsely chopped

1   unpeeled medium orange, coarsely chopped

¾   cup honey

1   (2½-pound) boneless pork roast

¼   cup honey

2   tablespoons Dijon mustard

2   tablespoons mixed peppercorns

½   teaspoon thyme

½   teaspoon salt

1   Combine the cranberries and orange in a saucepan and mix well. Stir in ¾ cup honey. Bring to a boil over medium-high heat, stirring occasionally. Boil for 3 to 4 minutes, stirring occasionally. Let stand until cool.

2   Make ½-inch slits over the surface of the roast. Combine ¼ cup honey, Dijon mustard, peppercorns, thyme and salt in a bowl and mix well. Brush ⅔ of the mixture over the roast. Place the roast on a rack in a roasting pan.

3   Bake at 300 degrees for 1 hour. Brush with the remaining honey-mustard. Bake for 45 minutes longer or until a meat thermometer registers 170 degrees. Serve with the cranberry relish.

SERVES 4 TO 6

BARBECUED RIBS

1   rack baby back pork ribs

½   cup catsup

¼   cup brown sugar (not packed)

¼   cup maple syrup

     juice of ½ orange

1   small onion, chopped

2   tablespoons soy sauce

1   tablespoon parsley flakes, or 2 tablespoons chopped fresh parsley

½   teaspoon pepper

1   Cut the ribs into 3-rib portions. Arrange in a baking dish. Combine the catsup, brown sugar, maple syrup, orange juice, onion, soy sauce, parsley flakes and pepper in a bowl and mix well. Pour over the ribs, turning to coat.

2   Marinate, covered, in the refrigerator for 8 hours or longer, turning occasionally. Bake, covered with foil, at 375 degrees for 45 minutes. Bake, uncovered, for 15 minutes longer until the ribs are cooked through or grill for a charcoal taste if desired.

SERVES 2

STUFFED PORK LOIN

1   **cup dried apricots**

1   **cup dried prunes**

1   **cup dried apples**

1   **cup dried cranberries**

    Cognac or bourbon

1   **cup whole cashews**

1   **(3- to 5-pound) boneless pork loin, trimmed, butterflied**

    Dijon mustard

    red cabbage leaves

    dry white wine

1   **jar red currant jelly**

½   **cup white wine**

2   **tablespoons (heaping) dry mustard**

1   Place the apricots, prunes, apples and cranberries in separate containers to preserve their colors. Pour enough Cognac over each of the dried fruits to cover. Let stand, covered, at room temperature for 24 hours, stirring occasionally. Drain, discarding the Cognac. Mix the fruits with the cashews in a bowl.

2   Pound the pork ¾ to 1 inch thick between sheets of plastic wrap. Spoon the fruit mixture over ⅓ of the pork. Roll as for a jelly roll to enclose the filling and secure with twine. Brush with Dijon mustard. Grill over medium-hot coals just long enough to sear.

3   Remove the roast to a baking pan lined with cabbage leaves. Cover the roast with additional cabbage leaves. Add enough white wine to the pan to reach halfway up the roast.

4   Roast at 350 degrees for about 1 hour or until a meat thermometer registers 170 degrees. Remove the roast to a cutting board, discarding the cabbage and wine. Let rest, covered, for 20 minutes. Cut into ¾-inch slices.

5   Heat the jelly in a saucepan until melted. Stir in the white wine and dry mustard. Serve with the pork.

SERVES 8 TO 10

Don't be afraid to mix patterns. If you're just beginning, try a floral, a plaid, and a mini-print or small paisley. Vary the scale and be sure colors are complementary.

JAMBALAYA

1	pound sausage, sliced
2	tablespoons vegetable oil
2	medium onions, chopped
1	cup chopped green onions
1	green bell pepper, chopped
2	garlic cloves, minced
1	teaspoon salt
¼	teaspoon black pepper
⅛	teaspoon cayenne pepper
1	cup uncooked rice
3	cups water

1 Brown the sausage in the oil in a heavy skillet; drain. Stir in the onions, green onions, green pepper and garlic. Cook over medium heat for 10 minutes, stirring occasionally. Stir in the salt, black pepper and cayenne pepper.

2 Combine the rice and water in a large saucepan. Bring to a boil. Stir in the sausage mixture. Cook over medium heat for 25 to 30 minutes or until the rice is tender, stirring occasionally.

SERVES 8

VEAL SPIEDINI

1½	pounds veal cutlets, thinly sliced
	salt and white pepper to taste
4	large onions, thinly sliced
½	cup olive oil
1	(10-ounce) package frozen green peas, thawed
6	ounces Stella Kasieri or Cascavallo cheese
1	bunch parsley, finely chopped
4	ounces pine nuts
	bread crumbs
	bay leaves
	olive oil

Great for buffets or day-after finger food for picnics.

1 Pound the veal cutlets into 3x6-inch portions between sheets of waxed paper. Sprinkle with salt and white pepper.

2 Sauté the onions in ½ cup olive oil until they are caramelized and light golden brown. Transfer the onion mixture to a large bowl. Stir in the green peas, cheese, parsley and pine nuts. Add enough bread crumbs to absorb the olive oil and bind the mixture.

3 Spoon some of the mixture into the center of each cutlet; roll to enclose the filling. Coat the rolls with bread crumbs. Arrange in an oiled 9x13-inch baking dish. Place bay leaves on the rolls and between each roll. Sprinkle with olive oil to taste. Bake at 325 degrees for 1¼ hours; discard the bay leaves.

SERVES 6 TO 8

VEAL RAGOUT

1 cup dry white wine

1 ounce dried porcini mushrooms, rinsed, patted dry

¼ cup mild olive oil

1 tablespoon unsalted butter

2 pounds leg of veal, cut into 1-inch cubes

12 large garlic cloves

2 tablespoons potato starch

1 cup dry white wine

3 tablespoons unsalted butter

1 cup rich chicken stock

½ cup loosely packed fresh sage

¼ cup chopped fresh Italian parsley

¼ cup crème de cassis

grated zest of 1 medium orange

salt and freshly ground pepper to taste

1 tablespoon red currant jelly

1 Heat 1 cup white wine in a saucepan until hot. Pour over the mushrooms in a bowl. Let stand for 1 hour.

2 Heat the olive oil and 1 tablespoon butter in a Dutch oven over high heat. Brown the veal in batches in the olive oil mixture. Remove to a bowl with a slotted spoon, reserving the pan drippings.

3 Sautè the garlic in the reserved pan drippings for 2 minutes. Add to the veal and mix well, discarding the pan drippings. Add the potato starch and toss to mix well.

4 Bring 1 cup white wine to a boil in the Dutch oven over high heat, stirring to deglaze the pan. Reduce the heat to low. Whisk in 3 tablespoons butter. Stir in the veal mixture, undrained mushrooms, stock, sage, parsley, crème de cassis, orange zest, salt and pepper. May be prepared to this point in advance and stored, covered, in the refrigerator until just before baking.

5 Bake, covered, for 40 minutes; remove cover. Bake for 35 to 40 minutes longer or until the veal is tender. Add the jelly, stirring until melted. Serve immediately.

SERVES 4 TO 6

Make an oversized runner for your dining room table. Measure width of table and add 20 inches or measure length of table and add 20 inches. Sew the two pieces of fabric back-to-back. If desired, stitch ends into chevron points; after turning, add a tassel to each point.

BARBECUED CHICKEN

½   cup water

¼   cup lemon juice

¼   cup vinegar

¼   cup olive oil

¼   cup Worcestershire sauce

¼   cup soy sauce

1   teaspoon each basil, pepper and dry mustard

1   bay leaf, crushed

1   garlic clove, finely chopped

    salt to taste

16 chicken pieces

1 Combine the water, lemon juice, vinegar, olive oil, Worcestershire sauce, soy sauce, basil, pepper, dry mustard, bay leaf, garlic and salt in a food processor container. Process until blended. Pour over the chicken in a large shallow dish, turning to coat.

2 Marinate the chicken, covered, in the refrigerator for 1 hour, turning once or twice. Drain, reserving the marinade.

3 Grill the chicken over low heat for 30 to 45 minutes or until the chicken is cooked through, turning and basting with the reserved marinade every 10 minutes.

SERVES 8

CHICKEN AND ZUCCHINI RISOTTO

2¾ cups chicken stock

1   yellow onion, chopped

¼   cup butter

1   cup uncooked Arborio rice

⅔   cup dry white wine

2   zucchini, cut into quarters lengthwise, cut into 1-inch pieces

1   (3-ounce) package sun-dried tomatoes, softened, chopped

2   cups chopped cooked chicken

½   cup freshly grated Parmesan cheese

2   tablespoons butter

1 Heat the chicken stock in a saucepan over low heat. Cover to keep warm. Sauté the onion in ¼ cup butter in a large saucepan over medium-high heat until tender and golden brown. Stir in the rice. Cook until the grains are coated, stirring constantly. Decrease the heat to medium. Stir in the white wine.

2 Cook until the wine is absorbed, stirring constantly. Add 1 cup of the stock and mix well. Cook until the stock is absorbed, stirring frequently. Add the remaining stock ½ cup at a time, cooking and stirring after each addition until the liquid is absorbed and the rice is tender. Stir in the zucchini, sun-dried tomatoes and chicken.

3 Cook until the zucchini is tender-crisp, stirring frequently. Add the cheese and 2 tablespoons butter and mix well.

SERVES 4 TO 6

LAZY CHICKEN DINNER

2   (3½- to 4-pound) roasting chickens, cut up

1   to 1¼ pounds small white onions

1   to 1¼ pounds new potatoes, peeled

1   pound carrots, peeled, cut into chunks

5   to 6 large garlic cloves, chopped

1½ to 2 teaspoons salt

1   teaspoon thyme, or 5 sprigs fresh thyme

    freshly ground pepper to taste

1   cup dry white wine

1   to 2 cups chicken stock

3   tablespoons unsalted butter

    chopped fresh parsley

1 Place the chicken in a 10x16-inch copper or enameled cast-iron baking pan. Arrange the onions, new potatoes and carrots around and on top of the chicken. Sprinkle with the garlic, salt, thyme and pepper. Pour the white wine and 1 cup of the stock over the chicken and vegetables. Dot with the butter.

2 Bake in the upper third of the oven at 500 degrees for 50 to 60 minutes or until the chicken is cooked through, turning and basting with the pan juices several times and adding the remaining 1 cup stock as needed; pan juices should be reduced by about ½. Sprinkle with parsley.

3 Reduce the oven temperature to 475 degrees if baking in a glass baking dish.

SERVES 6 TO 8

Take care to match the height of an end table with the height of a sofa or chair next to the table.

CHICKEN WITH MUSHROOM SAUCE

2	whole chicken breasts, split, boned
2	tablespoons flour
1/8	teaspoon pepper
2	tablespoons margarine
2	cups sliced fresh mushrooms
1/4	cup chopped onion
1	cup white wine
1/4	cup chopped fresh parsley
2	cups hot cooked rice or orzo

1 Coat the chicken with a mixture of the flour and pepper, shaking off and reserving the excess.

2 Brown the chicken on both sides in the margarine in a skillet over medium heat. Remove to a platter with a slotted spoon, reserving the pan drippings. Sauté the mushrooms and onion in the reserved pan drippings until tender and golden brown. Stir in the reserved flour mixture. Add the white wine. Bring to a boil, stirring frequently.

3 Return the chicken to the skillet. Stir in 2 tablespoons of the parsley. Simmer, covered, for 25 minutes. Spoon over the rice or pasta on a serving platter. Sprinkle with the remaining 2 tablespoons parsley.

SERVES 4

CHEESY CHICKEN CASSEROLE

8	ounces cream cheese, softened
1/2	cup (or more) milk
1/3	cup grated Parmesan cheese
1/2	teaspoon garlic salt, or to taste
6	to 8 chicken breasts, poached, chopped
1	(10-ounce) package frozen chopped broccoli, thawed, drained
	grated Parmesan cheese to taste

1 Combine the cream cheese, milk, 1/3 cup Parmesan cheese and garlic salt in a double boiler. Cook over hot water until blended and of a sauce consistency, stirring frequently and adding additional milk if needed for the desired consistency.

2 Layer the chicken, broccoli and cream cheese sauce 1/2 at a time in a baking dish. Sprinkle with Parmesan cheese to taste. Bake at 350 degrees for 25 to 30 minutes or until brown and bubbly.

SERVES 8 TO 10

Buffet Chicken

6   large garlic cloves, crushed

½   cup pitted prunes

¼   cup pitted green Spanish olives

¼   cup capers

3   bay leaves

¼   cup red wine vinegar

¼   cup olive oil

2   tablespoons oregano

    coarse salt and freshly ground pepper
    to taste

5   pounds chicken parts or boneless
    skinless chicken breasts

½   cup packed brown sugar

½   cup white wine

2   tablespoons finely chopped Italian
    parsley or cilantro

1   Combine the garlic, prunes, green olives, capers, bay leaves, wine vinegar, olive oil, oregano, salt and pepper in a large bowl and mix well. Add the chicken, tossing to coat. Marinate, covered, in the refrigerator for 8 to 10 hours, turning occasionally. Drain, reserving the marinade.

2   Arrange the chicken in a single layer in a large baking pan. Drizzle with the reserved marinade. Sprinkle with the brown sugar and drizzle with the white wine.

3   Bake at 350 degrees for 50 to 60 minutes or until cooked through, basting frequently with the pan drippings. Discard the bay leaves.

4   Transfer the chicken, prunes, olives and capers to a serving platter with a slotted spoon. Drizzle with some of the pan drippings. Sprinkle with the parsley. Serve immediately or at room temperature with the remaining pan juices.

SERVES 8

Make slipcovers for dining room chair seats. Add deep pleats or ruffles around three sides and fabric ties to attach to the back of the chair with a bow. Have slipcovers made for spring/summer, fall/winter, or holiday use.

LEMON CHICKEN

8	boneless chicken breast halves
	juice of 2½ lemons
1	cup flour
1	teaspoon salt
½	teaspoon paprika
¼	teaspoon pepper
2	tablespoons butter
1	tablespoon olive oil
¼	cup packed brown sugar
2	tablespoons grated lemon peel
2	tablespoons fresh lemon juice
2	tablespoons water
1	or 2 lemons, sliced

1 Combine the chicken and juice of 2½ lemons in a shallow dish, turning to coat. Marinate, covered, in the refrigerator for 8 to 10 hours, turning occasionally. Coat the chicken with a mixture of the flour, salt, paprika and pepper.

2 Melt the butter with the olive oil in a baking pan in a 425-degree oven. Decrease the oven temperature to 350 degrees. Arrange the chicken in a single layer in the prepared baking pan.

3 Sprinkle with a mixture of the brown sugar and lemon peel. Mix 2 tablespoons lemon juice and water in a measuring cup with lip. Pour over the chicken. Top with the lemon slices. Bake for 35 to 40 minutes or until the chicken is cooked through.

SERVES 8

CHICKEN WITH CASHEWS

3	tablespoons vegetable oil
2	boneless skinless chicken breasts, split, thinly sliced
2	garlic cloves, finely chopped
2	tablespoons soy sauce
1	tablespoon sherry
1	tablespoon cornstarch
¼	teaspoon ginger
1	medium green bell pepper, chopped
½	cup (or more) cashews

1 Microwave the oil on High in a microwave-safe dish for 2½ to 3 minutes. Mix the chicken, garlic, soy sauce, sherry, cornstarch and ginger in a bowl. Add to the hot oil.

2 Microwave on High for 3 to 4 minutes, stirring twice. Add the green pepper and cashews. Microwave, covered, for 2½ to 3 minutes or until the chicken is cooked through and the green pepper is tender, stirring once. Let stand for 3 minutes before serving.

SERVES 4

CHICKEN CHILI

12 boneless skinless chicken breasts, chopped

6 tablespoons olive oil

1 large onion, chopped

5 garlic cloves, minced

2 red bell peppers, chopped

4 jalapeño peppers, seeded, minced

3 tablespoons chili powder

1½ teaspoons cumin seeds

1 teaspoon coriander

⅛ teaspoon cinnamon

2 (16-ounce) cans whole tomatoes, chopped

1 cup sliced black olives

1 cup beer

¼ cup grated unsweetened chocolate

   salt to taste

You can't really taste the chocolate in this chili, but it adds a bit of tartness. It's also delicious without the chocolate.

1 Brown the chicken on all sides in 3 tablespoons of the olive oil in a large saucepan just until cooked through. Remove to a platter using a slotted spoon and reserving the pan drippings.

2 Heat the pan drippings and remaining 3 tablespoons olive oil over high heat. Stir in the onion and garlic. Sauté for 5 minutes. Stir in the red peppers and jalapeño peppers. Sauté over medium heat for 10 minutes.

3 Stir in the chili powder, cumin seeds, coriander and cinnamon. Cook for 5 minutes, stirring frequently. Add the chicken, undrained tomatoes, black olives and beer. Simmer over medium heat for 15 minutes, stirring occasionally. Add the chocolate and salt and mix well.

4 Ladle into chili bowls. Serve with chopped green onions, shredded Cheddar cheese, sour cream, chopped avocados and tortilla chips.

SERVES 6

Make "Santa sacks" for wine, home-made vinegars, or preserves by sewing two pieces of fabric together pillowcase-style. Pink top edges, turn, and tie closed with a tasseled chair tie.

ENCHILADAS MAÑANITAS

3 cups chopped cooked chicken, turkey or veal

1 cup chopped black olives

1 cup shredded Monterey Jack cheese

½ cup blanched slivered almonds

½ cup minced green onions

salt to taste

Enchilada Sauce

12 corn tortillas

1 cup shredded Monterey Jack cheese

sour cream

sliced green onions

chopped fresh cilantro

1 Combine the chicken, black olives, 1 cup cheese, almonds, green onions and salt in a bowl and mix well.

2 Heat the Enchilada Sauce in a saucepan until warm. Add the tortillas 1 at a time and let stand for 1 minute or until heated through. Remove the tortillas to a platter.

3 Spoon some of the chicken mixture in the center of each tortilla. Roll to enclose the filling. Arrange seam side down in a baking dish. Drizzle with the remaining Enchilada Sauce and sprinkle with 1 cup cheese. Chill until just before time to bake.

4 Bake at 350 degrees for 20 minutes or until the cheese is bubbly. Serve topped with sour cream, sliced green onions and chopped fresh cilantro.

MAKES 12 ENCHILADAS

Enchilada Sauce

1 large onion, chopped

½ cup chopped green bell pepper

1½ tablespoons vegetable oil

4½ cups tomato sauce or purée

1 tablespoon chili powder

salt to taste

1 Sauté the onion and green pepper in the oil in a saucepan until tender. Stir in the tomato sauce, chili powder and salt.

2 Simmer for 10 minutes or until of the desired consistency, stirring occasionally.

MAKES 6 CUPS

CHICKEN CURRY

1   large onion, chopped

3   ribs celery, chopped

3   tablespoons butter

3   tablespoons curry powder

1   teaspoon salt

3   cups chopped cooked chicken breast

1   (10-ounce) can cream of chicken soup

1   cup sour cream

¾   cup milk

      hot cooked brown rice

1   Sauté the onion and celery in the butter in a skillet for 5 minutes or until the vegetables are tender. Stir in 1 tablespoon of the curry powder and salt. Cook, covered, for 5 minutes, stirring occasionally. Stir in the chicken and 1 tablespoon of the remaining curry powder.

2   Cook, covered, for 5 minutes, stirring occasionally. Add the remaining 1 tablespoon curry powder, soup, sour cream and milk and mix well. Cook just until bubbly, stirring frequently. Spoon over the brown rice on a serving platter.

3   Serve with assorted condiments such as chopped green onions, chopped tomatoes, chopped apples, raisins, peanuts, mandarin oranges, shredded coconut and/or chutney.

SERVES 4 TO 6

To hang a carpet or oriental rug on the wall, nail tack-strip (used in upholstering furniture) to the wall and press the textile carefully onto the nails of the tack-strip.

SWEET-AND-SOUR CHICKEN

3   onions, chopped

4   carrots, julienned

1   green bell pepper, thinly sliced

1   garlic clove, minced

1   tablespoon vegetable oil

1   (6-ounce) can pineapple juice

¾   cup chicken broth

¾   cup light corn syrup

½   cup packed dark brown sugar

⅓   cup cider vinegar

¼   cup soy sauce

¼   cup catsup

3   tablespoons cornstarch

3   tablespoons water

1   (20-ounce) can pineapple chunks, drained

2   pounds boneless skinless chicken cutlets, cubed

½   cup milk

1   egg, beaten

1½   cups flour

½   teaspoon salt

2   to 3 tablespoons vegetable oil

1   Sauté the onions, carrots, green pepper and garlic in 1 tablespoon oil in a skillet over medium-high heat for 5 to 7 minutes or until tender-crisp.

2   Combine the pineapple juice, chicken broth, corn syrup, brown sugar, vinegar, soy sauce and catsup in a 4½-quart saucepan and mix well. Bring just to a boil over medium heat, stirring frequently. Add a mixture of the cornstarch and water gradually, cooking and stirring constantly until of the desired consistency. Stir in the pineapple and sautéed vegetables. Keep warm over low heat.

3   Dip the chicken in a mixture of the milk and egg. Coat with a mixture of the flour and salt. Fry in 2 to 3 tablespoons oil in a skillet over medium heat until golden brown and cooked through; drain. Add to the pineapple mixture and mix gently. Cook for 5 minutes or until heated through, stirring occasionally. Serve over steamed or fried rice.

SERVES 4 TO 5

GRILLED SALMON WITH SHRIMP

1   **(1-pound) salmon fillet**

1½   **tablespoons celery seeds**

1   **lemon, sliced**

4   **to 6 tablespoons butter or margarine, softened**

5   **ounces medium fresh shrimp, peeled, deveined**

1   **bunch fresh dillweed, trimmed**

1   Place the salmon in the center of a large sheet of heavy-duty foil. Sprinkle with the celery seeds. Arrange the lemon slices over the top and dot with butter. Cover with the shrimp. Top with the dillweed. Seal the foil tightly.

2   Grill over medium-low heat for 20 to 25 minutes or until the salmon flakes easily. Do not turn.

SERVES 2

SEAFOOD VERA CRUZ

2   **tablespoons olive oil**

1   **medium onion, sliced**

2   **green bell peppers, sliced**

2   **garlic cloves, crushed**

1   **tablespoon basil**

1   **teaspoon cumin**

1   **(16-ounce) can whole tomatoes**

1   **(6- to 8-ounce) halibut or other firm white fish fillets**

1   **to 2 cups shredded mozzarella cheese**

1   Heat a saucepan and add the olive oil, onion, green peppers, garlic, basil and cumin. Cook for 2 to 3 minutes, stirring constantly. Add the tomatoes, breaking up with a spoon. Cook for 7 to 10 minutes or until heated through.

2   Place the fish in an oiled baking pan. Pour the tomato mixture over the top and sprinkle with the cheese. Bake, covered, at 350 degrees for 10 to 20 minutes or until the fish flakes easily.

SERVES 4

EASTERN SHORE CRAB CAKES

1   pound lump crab meat

2   tablespoons mayonnaise

1   tablespoon dry mustard

1   egg, beaten

1   teaspoon salt

2   to 3 tablespoons butter

1 Combine the crab meat, mayonnaise, dry mustard, egg and salt in a bowl and mix gently. Shape into 4 patties.

2 Sauté the patties in the butter in a skillet over medium heat for 4 to 5 minutes on each side; drain. Serve with fresh sliced tomatoes and fresh corn.

MAKES 4 CRAB CAKES

CRAB IMPERIAL

1   tablespoon margarine

1   tablespoon flour

½   cup milk

1½   teaspoons Worcestershire sauce

1   teaspoon minced onion

2   slices white bread, crusts removed, cubed

½   cup mayonnaise

1   tablespoon lemon juice

½   teaspoon salt

⅛   to ¼ teaspoon pepper

2   tablespoons margarine

1   pound backfin crab meat, picked over

     paprika to taste

1 Melt 1 tablespoon margarine in a saucepan. Stir in the flour. Stir in the milk gradually. Cook over medium heat until thickened to sauce consistency, stirring constantly.

2 Add the Worcestershire sauce, onion and bread cubes and mix well. Let stand until cool. Fold in the mayonnaise, lemon juice, salt and pepper.

3 Heat 2 tablespoons margarine in a skillet until light brown. Add the crab meat and toss lightly with the margarine. Stir into the sauce. Spoon into a 1-quart baking dish. Sprinkle with paprika. Bake at 450 degrees for 10 to 15 minutes or until bubbly.

SERVES 4

CRAWFISH ÉTOUFFÉE

2   cups chopped onions

2   cups chopped celery

1   medium green bell pepper, chopped

2   garlic cloves, minced

½   cup butter or margarine

2   tablespoons flour

2   teaspoons Worcestershire sauce

1   teaspoon tomato purée

1   pound crawfish tails

1   cup water (optional)

½   cup chopped green onions

½   cup minced fresh parsley

     salt and pepper to taste

     Tabasco sauce to taste

When using fresh crawfish, include the bit of fat in the heads for flavor.

1   Sauté the onions, celery, green pepper and garlic in the butter in a large cast-iron skillet for about 30 minutes, stirring constantly. Add the flour and mix well. Stir in the Worcestershire sauce, tomato purée and crawfish tails.

2   Sauté for 5 minutes. Add the water if needed for the desired consistency. Stir in the green onions, parsley, salt, pepper and Tabasco sauce.

3   Simmer for 15 to 20 minutes, stirring frequently. Remove from the heat. Let stand for 20 to 30 minutes to improve the flavor. Serve over hot cooked rice.

SERVES 6

Invest in one great versatile tableskirt to really fit your table. Have it lined with a contrasting fabric; now you have two cloths as the beginning of a wardrobe for entertaining. Layer your investment basecloth with a smaller overcloth (square or round) and line that with a contrasting fabric again. If you're clever in fabric selection, you could have four looks in two reversible cloths!

TUNA STEAKS WITH SEAFOOD MAYONNAISE

1/3   cup virgin olive oil

1/3   cup fresh lemon juice

1/2   teaspoon coarsely ground pepper

8   (6-ounce) tuna steaks, 1 inch thick
       Seafood Mayonnaise

2   tablespoons chopped fresh flat-leaf
       parsley

1 1/2 tablespoons drained capers

1   tablespoon finely grated lemon zest

Great to prepare in advance for picnics or entertaining on hot summer nights.

1 Whisk the olive oil, lemon juice and pepper in a bowl. Pour over the tuna in a shallow dish, turning to coat. Marinate, covered, in the refrigerator for 30 minutes, turning once; drain.

2 Arrange the tuna on a broiler rack in a broiler pan. Broil 4 inches from the heat source for 4 to 5 minutes per side or until the tuna flakes easily. Cool to room temperature.

3 Arrange the tuna on a serving platter. Top each steak with 1/4 cup of the Seafood Mayonnaise. Sprinkle with the parsley, capers and lemon zest.

SERVES 8

Seafood Mayonnaise

1   egg

1   egg yolk

2 1/2 tablespoons fresh lemon juice

4   teaspoons Dijon mustard

1/2   cup olive oil

1/2   cup vegetable oil

1/2   cup drained canned tuna

1 1/2 tablespoons drained capers

4   flat anchovy fillets, drained

1   tablespoon fresh lemon juice

1/3   cup olive oil

2   teaspoons finely grated lemon zest

1/4   teaspoon coarsely ground pepper
       salt to taste

1 Process the egg, egg yolk, 2 1/2 tablespoons lemon juice and Dijon mustard in a food processor for 15 seconds. Add 1/2 cup olive oil and vegetable oil gradually, processing constantly until thickened and of mayonnaise consistency. Transfer to a bowl.

2 Process the tuna, capers, anchovies, 1 tablespoon lemon juice and 1/3 cup olive oil in a food processor for 1 minute or until smooth. Fold the tuna mixture into the mayonnaise. Add the lemon zest, pepper and salt and mix gently. Chill, covered, for 3 to 10 hours.

MAKES 2 CUPS

POINT BARROW SEAFOOD CASSEROLE

2   tablespoons butter

2   to 3 tablespoons flour

1   cup nondairy coffee creamer

1   cup low-fat milk

2   tablespoons sherry (optional)

2   tablespoons lemon juice

1   tablespoon Worcestershire sauce

1   tablespoon (rounded) catsup

½   teaspoon prepared mustard

½   teaspoon curry powder

½   teaspoon paprika

      salt to taste

      Tabasco sauce to taste

2½   pounds deveined peeled shrimp

1   pound lump crab meat

2   (14-ounce) cans artichoke hearts,
      drained, cut lengthwise into halves

1½   cups shredded sharp Cheddar cheese

2   (3-ounce) cans French-fried onions

1 Melt the butter in a heavy saucepan. Whisk in the flour until smooth. Add the coffee creamer and low-fat milk gradually, stirring constantly. Cook until thickened and of sauce consistency, stirring constantly. Add the sherry, lemon juice, Worcestershire sauce, catsup, prepared mustard, curry powder, paprika, salt and Tabasco sauce and mix well. Cook just until blended, stirring constantly.

2 Layer the shrimp, crab meat, artichokes and sauce in a 10x14-inch baking dish. Sprinkle with the cheese.

3 Bake at 350 degrees for 20 minutes. Turn off the oven. Sprinkle with the onions. Let stand in the closed oven until the onions are crisp.

4 The flavor of this dish is enhanced if the casserole is prepared 1 day in advance, stored covered in the refrigerator and baked just before serving. You may substitute 3 pounds imitation lump crab meat for the crab meat and shrimp.

SERVES 10

Add texture to your tablesetting, using
items such as woven placemats,
textured napkins, and wood flatware.

ASPARAGUS AND CASHEW STIR-FRY

1½ pounds fresh asparagus, trimmed

2 tablespoons olive oil

2 teaspoons sesame oil

1 tablespoon finely chopped gingerroot

½ cup coarsely chopped cashews, toasted

1 tablespoon soy sauce

1 Cut each asparagus stalk diagonally into 2 or 3 portions. Heat the olive oil and sesame oil in a wok or skillet over medium heat until hot.

2 Add the gingerroot to the wok. Stir-fry for 1 minute. Add the asparagus. Stir-fry for 4 to 5 minutes or until tender-crisp. Stir in the cashews and soy sauce. Serve immediately.

SERVES 6

Those of us with round dining tables like to entertain with a wardrobe of tableskirts. Use a floor-length basecloth in a basic color such as rose, azure, gold, or green. Then have several different square toppers made for the way you like to entertain: in holiday colors, summer brights or cabaña stripes for casual evenings, damask prints for dinner parties—you get the idea!

RED BEANS AND RICE

4	slices smoked bacon, chopped
¼	cup olive oil
1	medium onion, chopped
1	medium green bell pepper, chopped
2	garlic cloves, crushed
1	cup water
3	tablespoons tomato paste
2	(16-ounce) cans red kidney beans
1	envelope Goya Sazon seasoning
1½	teaspoons salt
⅛	teaspoon pepper
2	cups cooked white rice

1 Fry the bacon in a skillet just until cooked through. Remove and drain, reserving about 1 teaspoon of the bacon drippings. Heat the reserved bacon drippings and olive oil in a skillet.

2 Add the onion, green pepper and garlic to the skillet. Sauté until the vegetables are tender. Stir in the water and tomato paste. Add the bacon, undrained beans, Goya Sazon seasoning, salt and pepper and mix well. Simmer for 30 minutes, stirring occasionally. Serve over the rice.

SERVES 4

TUSCAN-STYLE BEANS

2	ounces prosciutto or pancetta, finely chopped
1	small onion, sliced
3	garlic cloves, minced
½	cup olive oil
8	fresh sage leaves, chopped
2	(16-ounce) cans cannellini beans, rinsed, drained
	salt and pepper to taste

1 Sauté the prosciutto, onion and garlic in 1 tablespoon of the olive oil in a skillet for 8 to 10 minutes or until the onion is tender. Stir in the sage.

2 Cook for 1 minute, stirring constantly. Add the remaining olive oil, beans, salt and pepper and mix gently. Cook just until heated through, stirring occasionally. Garnish with additional sage leaves.

SERVES 4 TO 6

BROCCOLI SUPREME

2   large bunches broccoli, trimmed

     salt to taste

1   cup Crème Fraîche

⅔   cup grated Parmesan cheese

¼   cup sour cream

½   teaspoon freshly grated nutmeg

½   teaspoon freshly ground pepper

2   tablespoons unsalted butter

This dish holds up better than fresh broccoli for large dinner parties and can be prepared in advance.

1   Peel the broccoli stems. Reserve 8 small broccoli florets. Chop the remaining broccoli and stems. Combine the reserved whole florets, chopped broccoli and chopped stems with enough boiling salted water to cover in a large saucepan. Cook for 8 minutes or until tender-crisp; drain. Set aside the 8 whole florets.

2   Combine the chopped broccoli and chopped stems with the Crème Fraîche in a food processor container and process until puréed. Combine the purée, cheese, sour cream, nutmeg, pepper and salt to taste in a bowl and mix well.

3   Spoon into a baking dish. Dot with the butter. Bake at 350 degrees for 25 minutes or until heated through. Top with the reserved florets. Serve immediately.

SERVES 8

Crème Fraîche

1   cup whipping cream

1   cup sour cream

1   Whisk the whipping cream and sour cream in a bowl until blended. Let stand, loosely covered with plastic wrap, in a warm environment for 8 to 10 hours or until thickened.

2   Chill, covered, for 4 hours or longer before using.

MAKES 2 CUPS

BROCCOLI AND FENNEL

florets of 1½ pounds broccoli

salt to taste

1 tablespoon butter

1 tablespoon vegetable oil

8 ounces fennel, thinly sliced

2 garlic cloves, minced

½ teaspoon salt

1 tablespoon lemon juice

⅛ teaspoon red pepper flakes (optional)

1 Combine the broccoli with ¼ inch salted boiling water in a skillet. Cook for 3 to 5 minutes or until tender-crisp; drain and reserve.

2 Heat the butter and oil in a skillet over medium-high heat until the butter melts. Add the fennel, garlic and ½ teaspoon salt. Cook, covered, over low heat for 8 minutes or until the fennel is tender, stirring occasionally. Stir in the broccoli, lemon juice and red pepper flakes. Cook for 2 minutes or until heated through, stirring occasionally.

SERVES 4

CARROT SOUFFLÉ

2 cups cooked carrots

¼ cup honey

1 teaspoon salt

1½ cups light cream or half-and-half

3 tablespoons cornstarch

3 eggs, beaten

¼ cup melted butter

This is just as good cold the next day!

1 Process the carrots, honey, salt and ¾ cup of the cream in a blender until smooth. Mix the remaining ¾ cup cream and cornstarch in a small bowl. Add to the blender with the eggs and butter and process until smooth.

2 Spoon into a greased 1½- or 2-quart baking dish. Bake at 400 degrees for 45 to 55 minutes or until set.

SERVES 8

CORN AND TOMATO GRATIN

2   cups chopped seeded tomatoes, drained

    salt and pepper to taste

1½ cups chopped onions

2   tablespoons olive oil

5   cups fresh corn kernels, cut from 7 ears

⅛   teaspoon nutmeg

2½ cups half-and-half

3   eggs

2   egg whites

½   teaspoon hot pepper sauce

½   cup chopped fresh basil

You can substitute the equivalent amount of egg substitute for the eggs and egg whites in this recipe.

1 Sprinkle the tomatoes with salt and pepper in a colander and let stand to drain.

2 Sauté the onions in the olive oil in a skillet over medium-high heat for 4 minutes or until tender. Stir in the corn. Sauté for 6 minutes or until tender. Add the nutmeg and season with salt and pepper. Let stand until cool.

3 Whisk the half-and-half, eggs, egg whites and hot pepper sauce in a bowl until blended. Stir in the corn mixture.

4 Spoon into a 2-quart baking dish sprayed with nonstick cooking spray. Bake at 350 degrees for 30 minutes or until set. Sprinkle the tomatoes over the top. Bake for 8 minutes longer or until the tomatoes are heated through. Sprinkle with the basil.

SERVES 6

If you use a round table as an end table or bedside table, have a reversible tableskirt made in a floor-length base-cloth. Use two complementary colors, but make one lighter for spring/summer and one darker for fall/winter. A square or round topper can also be reversible so that you can have three or four looks in one table.

MUSHROOMS BERKELEY

2   tablespoons Dijon mustard

2   tablespoons Worcestershire sauce

½   cup packed brown sugar

¾   cup red wine

     seasoned salt and freshly ground pepper to taste

1   onion, chopped

½   cup butter

1   pound fresh mushrooms, cut into halves

2   medium green bell peppers, cut into 1-inch pieces

1 Combine the Dijon mustard, Worcestershire sauce, brown sugar and wine in a bowl and mix until smooth. Season with salt and pepper.

2 Sauté the onion in the butter in a large saucepan until transparent. Add the mushrooms and green peppers. Sauté until the mushrooms begin to brown. Stir in the wine sauce.

3 Simmer over medium heat for 45 minutes or until the liquid is reduced and thickened; mushrooms will be quite dark and flavorful.

SERVES 6

MEXICAN CORN PUDDING

2   medium onions, chopped

1   cup melted butter

3   eggs, beaten

1   cup milk

½   cup buttermilk

1   cup yellow cornmeal

1½ cups cooked fresh or frozen corn

1½ tablespoons chopped jalapeño peppers

1   cup shredded Monterey Jack cheese

1   cup shredded sharp Cheddar cheese

1 Sauté the onions in ½ cup of the butter in a skillet until tender. Whisk the remaining ½ cup butter, eggs, milk and buttermilk in a bowl. Stir in the onions, cornmeal, corn and jalapeño peppers. Add half the Monterey Jack cheese and Cheddar cheese and mix gently.

2 Spoon into a buttered 9x9-inch baking dish. Sprinkle with the remaining cheeses. Bake at 350 degrees for 45 minutes. Cool slightly before serving.

SERVES 8 TO 10

POTATO PIEROGIES

4 **cups flour**

1 **teaspoon salt**

1½ **cups lukewarm water**

2 **tablespoons vegetable oil**

1 **egg, beaten**

6 **medium potatoes, peeled, cut into quarters**

1 **cup cottage cheese**

  salt and pepper to taste

  melted margarine

For variety, substitute Granny Smith apples for the potatoes and sprinkle with sugar.

1 Mix the flour and salt in a bowl. Whisk the lukewarm water, oil and egg in a bowl. Add to the flour mixture gradually, mixing to form a dough; cover and set aside.

2 Combine the potatoes with enough water to cover in a saucepan. Cook until tender; drain. Mash the potatoes. Let stand until cool. Stir in the cottage cheese. Season with salt and pepper.

3 Roll the dough the thickness of pie pastry on a lightly floured surface. Cut into 3-inch circles with a biscuit cutter. Spoon 1 tablespoon of the potato mixture into the center of each circle and fold over to enclose the filling. Pinch the edges to seal. Place on a sheet of waxed paper sprinkled lightly with flour.

4 Bring a stockpot of salted water to a boil. Drop the pierogies 1 at a time into the water and stir gently. Boil for 5 minutes or until the pierogies float to the top. Drain on paper towels.

5 Transfer to a serving platter. Drizzle with margarine, turning to coat. Serve immediately or panfry with onions until golden brown. Serve with sour cream.

6 Pierogies may be prepared, layered between sheets of waxed paper and frozen for future use. Reheat by boiling or panfrying.

MAKES 40 PIEROGIES

GRILLED POTATO AND ONION PACKETS

⅔   cup olive oil

6   tablespoons chopped fresh thyme, or 3 tablespoons dried thyme

1   tablespoon Dijon mustard

1   teaspoon salt

1   teaspoon pepper

2   pounds white potatoes, peeled, cut into ¼-inch slices

2   medium red onions, cut into ¼-inch slices

     salt and pepper to taste

This dish can also be baked in a covered baking dish at 350 degrees for 30 minutes. Bake, uncovered, for 5 minutes to brown.

1 Whisk the olive oil, 6 tablespoons thyme, Dijon mustard, 1 teaspoon salt and 1 teaspoon pepper in a bowl. Add the potatoes and red onions, tossing to coat.

2 Cut six 9x18-inch sheets of heavy-duty foil. Spray with nonstick cooking spray. Spoon the potato mixture in the centers of the foil sheets. Sprinkle with salt and pepper. Seal the foil tightly.

3 Place the foil packets on the grill over medium-high heat. Grill for 25 minutes, turning occasionally, or until the potatoes are tender and golden brown. Slit top of foil and garnish with sprigs of fresh thyme.

SERVES 6

PEPPER RATATOUILLE

2   large yellow onions, thinly sliced

1   cup olive oil

12   large garlic cloves, thinly sliced

2   large unpeeled eggplant

2   red bell peppers, coarsely chopped

2   green bell peppers, coarsely chopped

8   jalapeño peppers, seeded, minced

4   yellow squash, chopped

2   tablespoons oregano

4   teaspoons cumin

48   cherry tomatoes, cut into halves

6   tablespoons chopped cilantro

1 Sauté the onions in the olive oil in a stockpot over medium-high heat for 10 minutes. Stir in the garlic. Sauté for 5 minutes.

2 Cut the eggplant into 1-inch cubes. Add to the saucepan and mix well. Cook over medium heat for 15 minutes, stirring occasionally. Add the red peppers, green peppers, jalapeño peppers and yellow squash and mix well. Stir in the oregano and cumin. Simmer, covered, over medium-low heat for 25 minutes, stirring occasionally.

3 Add the cherry tomatoes. Simmer for 10 minutes, stirring occasionally. Serve hot or at room temperature topped with the chopped cilantro.

SERVES 12

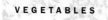

RATATOUILLE

1   **pound unpeeled eggplant, cut into ½-inch pieces**

1   **tablespoon kosher salt**

1   **medium onion, chopped**

¼   **cup olive oil**

2   **garlic cloves, minced**

2   **medium zucchini or yellow squash, chopped**

1   **red bell pepper, chopped**

1   **green bell pepper, chopped**

½   **cup olive oil**

2   **cups drained canned tomatoes, seeded, chopped**

½   **cup minced fresh parsley**

½   **cup minced fresh basil**

1   **teaspoon dried oregano**

      freshly ground pepper to taste

1   Toss the eggplant with the salt in a bowl. Set aside.

2   Sauté the onion in ¼ cup olive oil in a skillet for 5 minutes or until tender. Stir in the garlic. Sauté for 5 minutes. Add the zucchini, red pepper, green pepper and ½ cup olive oil and mix well. Simmer for 5 minutes, stirring frequently.

3   Squeeze the excess moisture from the eggplant. Add to the zucchini mixture and mix well. Stir in the tomatoes, parsley, basil, oregano and pepper. Simmer, covered, for 30 minutes, stirring occasionally. Serve at room temperature.

SERVES 4 TO 6

Instead of placemats, consider using two long runners that cross on the table to create a special background for your place settings. When they're custom-made, you can get the perfect length, color, and texture.

ROASTED TOMATO AND BASIL CASSEROLE

¾ cup chopped fresh basil

½ cup chopped fresh Italian parsley

2½ tablespoons chopped fresh oregano

3 medium onions, thinly sliced,
separated into rings

Dijon Vinaigrette

8 to 10 large tomatoes, thickly sliced,
drained

3 tablespoons bread crumbs

3 tablespoons freshly grated Parmesan
cheese

The Dijon Vinaigrette used here can also be tossed with a green salad.

1 Mix the basil, parsley and oregano in a bowl. Spread half the onions in an 8x12-inch baking dish. Drizzle with 1 tablespoon of the Dijon Vinaigrette. Layer with half the tomatoes. Drizzle with 1 tablespoon of the vinaigrette. Sprinkle with half the basil mixture.

2 Repeat the layering process. Drizzle with the remaining vinaigrette. Top with a mixture of the bread crumbs and cheese. Bake at 375 degrees for 1 hour.

SERVES 6 TO 8

Dijon Vinaigrette

¼ cup olive oil

2 tablespoons white wine vinegar

2 teaspoons Dijon mustard

2 garlic cloves, minced

¼ teaspoon sugar

¼ teaspoon salt

¼ teaspoon freshly ground pepper

1 Mix the olive oil, wine vinegar, Dijon mustard, garlic, sugar, salt and pepper in a jar with a tightfitting lid. Cover the jar and shake to mix.

2 Store in the refrigerator until needed.

MAKES ½ CUP

SWEET POTATO CASSEROLE

2   large or 3 medium unpeeled sweet
    potatoes

⅓   cup sugar

½   cup butter, softened

⅓   cup milk

2   eggs, beaten

1   teaspoon vanilla extract

⅓   cup packed brown sugar

¼   cup flour

¼   cup (scant) melted butter

½   cup chopped pecans

1   Combine the sweet potatoes with enough water to cover in a saucepan. Cook for 30 minutes or until tender; drain and cool slightly. Peel the sweet potatoes and mash.

2   Combine with the sugar, softened butter, milk, eggs and vanilla in a mixer bowl. Beat until fluffy. Spoon into a 9x13-inch baking dish.

3   Mix the brown sugar, flour, melted butter and pecans in a bowl. Sprinkle over the casserole. Bake at 325 degrees for 30 minutes.

SERVES 4 TO 6

RUM-SPICED YAMS

5   to 6 pounds yams

½   to 1 cup milk

½   cup sugar

¼   to ½ cup dark rum

¼   to ½ cup brandy

3   to 6 tablespoons butter, softened

1   teaspoon cinnamon

½   teaspoon nutmeg

½   teaspoon ground cloves

½   teaspoon salt

½   cup packed brown sugar

¼   cup finely chopped pecans or walnuts

This is sure to become a tradition at Thanksgiving and Christmas. The yams can be prepared well in advance of the holiday meal.

1   Arrange the yams on a baking sheet. Bake at 375 degrees for 45 to 60 minutes or until very tender. Let stand until cool. Peel the yams.

2   Beat the yams in a mixer bowl until smooth. Stir in the milk, sugar, rum, brandy, butter, cinnamon, nutmeg, cloves and salt. Spoon into a baking dish.

3   Mix the brown sugar and pecans in a bowl. Sprinkle over the yams. Bake at 400 degrees for 30 minutes or until heated through.

SERVES 8 TO 10

VEGETARIAN CHILI

2½ cups dried kidney beans

1 cup tomato juice

1 cup uncooked bulgur

2 cups chopped onions

6 to 8 large garlic cloves, minced

1 carrot, chopped

1 medium rib celery, chopped

2 teaspoons cumin

2 teaspoons basil

2 teaspoons chili powder

1½ teaspoons salt

black pepper to taste

cayenne pepper to taste

2 tablespoons olive oil

1 medium green bell pepper, chopped

1 (15-ounce) can diced tomatoes

3 tablespoons tomato paste

chopped fresh parsley and/or shredded cheese

1   Rinse and sort the beans. Soak in water to cover in a bowl for 8 to 10 hours; drain. Combine with fresh water to cover in a large saucepan. Bring to a boil and reduce the heat. Simmer, loosely covered, until tender; drain.

2   Bring the tomato juice to a boil in a saucepan. Add to the bulgur in a bowl and mix well. Let stand, covered, for 15 minutes. Stir into the beans.

3   Sauté the onions, half the garlic, carrot, celery, cumin, basil, chili powder, salt, black pepper and cayenne pepper in the olive oil in a skillet over medium heat for 5 minutes. Stir in the green pepper. Sauté until the vegetables are tender. Add to the bean mixture with the undrained tomatoes and tomato paste and mix well.

4   Simmer for 15 minutes, stirring occasionally. Stir in the remaining garlic. Simmer for 5 to 15 minutes longer or until of the desired consistency, stirring occasionally. Sprinkle servings with parsley and/or cheese.

SERVES 6

Stuffed Zucchini

1   cup small shell macaroni

2   (10-inch) zucchini

¼   cup olive oil

1   onion, chopped

4   garlic cloves, minced

2   tomatoes, peeled, seeded, chopped

1   cup shredded Cheddar cheese

2   tablespoons minced fresh parsley

1   teaspoon oregano

     salt and freshly ground pepper
     to taste

¼   cup freshly grated Parmesan cheese

1   Cook the macaroni in boiling water to cover in a saucepan for 5 minutes, stirring occasionally; drain.

2   Cut each zucchini lengthwise into halves. Remove the pulp carefully, leaving a ¼-inch shell. Brush the inside of the shells with half the olive oil. Chop enough of the pulp to measure 2 cups.

3   Cook the zucchini pulp, onion and garlic in the remaining 2 tablespoons olive oil in a skillet over medium heat, stirring frequently; drain. Add the macaroni, tomatoes, Cheddar cheese, parsley, oregano, salt and pepper and mix well.

4   Spoon into the zucchini shells. Arrange in a shallow baking dish. Add ½ inch water to the dish.

5   Bake, covered with foil, at 350 degrees for 30 minutes or until the zucchini is tender. Remove the foil and drain any remaining water. Sprinkle with the Parmesan cheese. Broil until bubbly.

6   Add browned Italian sausage to the zucchini mixture to serve as a main dish.

SERVES 4

Rearrange the furniture in the fall: draw the sofa up to the fireplace and stack magazines and books you've been meaning to read nearby. Be sure there are BIG pillows on the sofa (18 inches to 24 inches) so that you can really nestle in for a comfy read.

VEGETABLE CASSEROLE

1   (10-ounce) package frozen French-style green beans

1   (10-ounce) package frozen baby lima beans

1   (10-ounce) package frozen small green peas

3   green bell peppers, julienned

1½ cups whipping cream, whipped

1½ cups mayonnaise

¾   cup grated Parmesan cheese

     salt and pepper to taste

1 Combine the green beans, lima beans, green peas and green peppers with a small amount of boiling water in a saucepan. Cook just until thawed and separated; drain. Let stand until cool. Spoon into a buttered 2- or 3-quart baking dish.

2 Mix the whipped cream, mayonnaise, cheese, salt and pepper in a bowl. Spoon over the vegetables; do not stir. Bake at 325 degrees for 50 minutes or until puffed and light brown.

SERVES 8 TO 10

MEXICAN GRITS

1   cup instant grits, cooked

1   cup shredded sharp Cheddar cheese

1   (4-ounce) can chopped green chiles, drained

⅓   cup melted butter

2   eggs, beaten

1   garlic clove, minced

½   teaspoon salt

½   teaspoon black pepper

¼   teaspoon Tabasco sauce

¼   teaspoon white pepper

     shredded Cheddar cheese to taste

     paprika to taste

1 Combine the grits, 1 cup cheese, chiles, butter, eggs, garlic, salt, black pepper, Tabasco sauce and white pepper in a bowl and mix well. Spoon into a baking dish.

2 Sprinkle with cheese and paprika. Bake at 350 degrees for 1 hour.

SERVES 6

CHAMPAGNE RICE PILAF

1½ cups uncooked long grain white rice

¼ cup white sesame seeds

1½ cups Champagne

1 cup chicken broth

1 tablespoon light soy sauce

1 teaspoon freshly grated nutmeg

½ teaspoon Chinese chili sauce

½ teaspoon salt

¼ teaspoon ground cloves

4 garlic cloves, minced

2 shallots, minced

3 tablespoons unsalted butter

1 cup dark raisins

1 red bell pepper, chopped

½ cup minced green onions

⅓ cup chopped fresh basil

1 Rinse the rice with cold water in a sieve for 2 minutes or until the rinse water is no longer cloudy, stirring constantly; drain. Toast the sesame seeds in a small ungreased skillet for 2 minutes or until light golden brown. Remove immediately to a small bowl.

2 Mix the Champagne, broth, soy sauce, nutmeg, chili sauce, salt and cloves in a bowl and set aside.

3 Sauté the garlic and shallots in the butter in a 3-quart saucepan over medium-high heat until the butter sizzles. Add the rice, stirring to coat well. Sauté for 5 minutes or until heated through, stirring frequently. Add the raisins and Champagne mixture and mix well. Bring just to a boil and reduce the heat.

4 Simmer, covered, for 18 to 25 minutes or until all of the liquid is absorbed and the rice is tender. Stir in the red pepper, green onions, basil and sesame seeds. Serve immediately.

5 The rice may be prepared in advance and stored, covered, in the refrigerator until just before serving time. Reheat at 325 degrees for 15 minutes. Stir in the red pepper, green onions, basil and sesame seeds just before serving.

SERVES 6

It's great to mix patterns and prints in a room—but remember that the eye also needs a place to rest. Add some solid textures to a room with multiple patterns to provide a little visual relief.

LEMON RICE

2½ cups chicken broth

½ teaspoon salt

1 garlic clove, crushed

1 cup uncooked long grain rice

1 tablespoon finely grated lemon zest

2 tablespoons chopped fresh dillweed

2 tablespoons unsalted butter, softened

freshly ground pepper to taste

A great accompaniment for fish.

1 Bring the broth, salt and garlic to a boil in a saucepan. Stir in the rice. Simmer, covered, for 20 minutes or until the liquid is absorbed. Remove from the heat.

2 Stir in the lemon zest. Let stand, covered, for 5 minutes. Add the dillweed and butter, stirring until the butter melts. Season with pepper. Serve immediately.

SERVES 4 TO 6

MINTED WILD RICE

1 cup wild rice, rinsed

5½ cups (or less) low-fat chicken stock or water

1 cup pecan halves

1 cup golden raisins

grated peel of 1 large orange

¼ cup chopped fresh mint

4 green onions, thinly sliced

¼ cup olive oil

⅓ cup orange juice

1 teaspoon salt

freshly ground pepper to taste

Minted Wild Rice is a very good buffet dish.

1 Bring the rice and stock to a boil in a saucepan and reduce the heat. Simmer for 30 to 45 minutes or until tender; drain.

2 Combine with the pecans, raisins, orange peel, mint, green onions, olive oil, orange juice, salt and pepper in a bowl and mix well. Let stand at room temperature for 2 hours. Serve at room temperature.

SERVES 6

WILD RICE WITH PECANS

2 tablespoons butter or margarine

2 (6-ounce) packages long grain and wild rice mix with seasoning packets

4 cups chicken broth

8 green onions, chopped

8 medium mushrooms, sliced

1½ cups chopped pecans, toasted

1 Melt the butter in a large saucepan. Stir in the rice. Sauté over medium heat until light brown. Add the seasoning packets, broth, green onions and mushrooms and mix well. Bring to a boil.

2 Pour into a lightly greased 3-quart baking dish. Bake, covered, at 350 degrees for 30 minutes; remove the cover. Bake for 30 minutes longer or until the rice is tender and the liquid is absorbed, stirring after 15 minutes. Add the pecans and mix well. Serve immediately.

SERVES 12

BULGUR PILAF

1 small onion, finely chopped

1 garlic clove, finely chopped

3 tablespoons butter or margarine

1 cup uncooked bulgur or brown rice

1 (10-ounce) can consommé

1 cup chablis or other white wine

½ teaspoon salt

⅓ cup pine nuts, chopped fresh parsley or finely sliced green onions (optional)

Good with game hens, lamb, or beef.

1 Sauté the onion and garlic in the butter in a saucepan until the onion is tender but not brown. Add the bulgur and mix well. Cook for several minutes, stirring constantly. Stir in the consommé, wine and salt. Bring to a boil.

2 Spoon into a baking dish. Bake, tightly covered, at 350 degrees for 45 to 60 minutes or until the liquid is absorbed and the bulgur is tender, stirring occasionally. Stir in the pine nuts, parsley or green onions.

SERVES 4 TO 5

AÏOLI

3 egg yolks

1 tablespoon Dijon mustard

1 medium head garlic, crushed

1½ cups extra-virgin olive oil

juice of 1 lemon

1 teaspoon dried basil or tarragon, or
2 tablespoons chopped fresh basil
or tarragon

salt to taste

Serve as an accompaniment to vegetables and fish or spread on fresh salmon fillets before broiling or grilling.

1 Process the egg yolks, Dijon mustard and garlic in a food processor until blended. Add the olive oil gradually, processing constantly until thickened. Add the lemon juice, basil and salt. Process until smooth.

2 Store, covered, in the refrigerator for up to 2 weeks.

MAKES 2 TO 3 CUPS

SPICED CRANBERRIES

1½ cups sugar

¾ cup water

2 (3-inch) cinnamon sticks

3 whole cloves

3 whole allspice

1 (12- to 16-ounce) package fresh cranberries

zest of 1 large orange

2 to 3 tablespoons Grand Marnier

1 Bring the sugar, water, cinnamon sticks, cloves and allspice to a boil in a saucepan. Boil until the sugar dissolves, stirring occasionally. Stir in the cranberries.

2 Cook until the cranberries pop, stirring occasionally. Remove from the heat. Stir in the orange zest and Grand Marnier. Cool slightly. Chill, covered, for 24 hours. Discard the cinnamon sticks, cloves and allspice before serving.

SERVES 10 TO 12

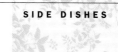

CRANBERRY ORANGE RELISH

4   **cups whole cranberries**

1   **unpeeled orange, seeded, chopped**

1   **unpeeled apple, chopped**

½   **cup crushed pineapple**

2   **cups sugar, or to taste**

½   **teaspoon nutmeg**

1   Process the cranberries, orange and apple separately in a food processor until coarsely chopped; do not purée.

2   Combine the cranberries, orange, apple and pineapple in a bowl and mix gently. Stir in the sugar and nutmeg. Store, covered, in the refrigerator.

MAKES 4 CUPS

BREAD-AND-BUTTER PICKLES

1   **quart thinly sliced cucumbers**

6   **medium white onions, thinly sliced**

1   **green bell pepper, thinly sliced**

1   **red bell pepper, thinly sliced**

3   **garlic cloves**

⅓   **cup salt**

5   **cups sugar**

3   **cups white vinegar**

2   **tablespoons mustard seeds**

1½   **teaspoons turmeric**

1½   **teaspoons celery seeds**

1   Layer the cucumbers, onions, green bell pepper, red bell pepper and garlic in a crock, sprinkling the salt between the layers. Cover with ice cubes. Let stand at room temperature for 3 hours. Drain, discarding the salt water. Transfer the cucumber mixture to a stockpot.

2   Combine the sugar, vinegar, mustard seeds, turmeric and celery seeds in a bowl and mix well. Pour over the cucumber mixture and mix gently. Bring just to a boil.

3   Pack the cucumber mixture into hot sterilized jars. Add the boiling syrup, leaving a ½-inch headspace. Seal with 2-piece lids. Let stand for 1 month before serving.

MAKES 8 PINTS

PASTA

MEXICAN BOW TIES

1   (32-ounce) package farfalle, or
      bow tie pasta

1   pound onions, chopped

2   cups chopped green bell peppers

3   cups coarsely chopped tomatoes

5   teaspoons minced garlic

3   tablespoons minced jalapeño
      peppers

1¼ cups chopped fresh cilantro

1   cup grated Parmesan cheese

1   cup olive oil

3   tablespoons lime juice

2   teaspoons salt

      freshly ground black pepper to taste

You may add chopped cooked chicken or sausage to this and serve it hot as a main dish.

1   Cook the pasta in simmering water in a saucepan for 12 minutes; drain and cool.

2   Combine the onions, green peppers, tomatoes, garlic, jalapeño peppers, cilantro and cheese in a salad bowl. Add the olive oil, lime juice, salt and black pepper and toss to coat well. Add the pasta and mix well.

SERVES 10

If it's important for you to use armcovers on upholstered furniture, baste them on so that they can't move. An alternative is to use clear twist pins to anchor them at the base on the arm of the furniture.

BOW TIE CHICKEN AND VEGETABLE SALAD

1   (16-ounce) package bow tie pasta

4   ounces snow peas

12   stalks asparagus

6   green onions, finely chopped

2   tablespoons grated fresh ginger

2   cups chopped cooked chicken
      Hoisin Dressing

1   Cook the pasta using the package directions; drain and rinse with cold water.

2   Blanch the snow peas in boiling water in a saucepan for 30 to 60 seconds; refresh in ice water and drain. Cut into julienne strips. Blanch the asparagus in boiling water in a saucepan for 1 to 2 minutes; refresh in ice water and drain. Cut into 1/2-inch pieces.

3   Combine the pasta, snow peas, asparagus, green onions, ginger and chicken in a salad bowl and mix well. Chill, covered, until serving time. Add the Hoisin Dressing and toss to coat well.

SERVES 4

Hoisin Dressing

1/3   cup hoisin sauce

1/4   cup soy sauce

1/4   cup balsamic vinegar

2   teaspoons Dijon mustard
     juice of 1 lime

2/3   cup vegetable oil

1   Combine the hoisin sauce, soy sauce, vinegar and mustard in a blender container. Add the lime juice and process until smooth.

2   Add the vegetable oil gradually, processing constantly. Chill until serving time.

MAKES 1 1/2 CUPS

CAESAR PASTA SALAD

1   (16-ounce) package rotini

½   cup chopped green bell pepper

½   cup chopped red bell pepper

½   cup chopped unpeeled cucumber

¼   cup sliced green olives

¼   cup sliced black olives

1   (14-ounce) can artichoke hearts,
       drained, cut into quarters

1   avocado, chopped

½   cup sliced mild green chile peppers

3   green onions, chopped

1   cup drained cooked small shrimp

4   ounces sliced pepperoni, cut into
       halves

½   cup grated Parmesan cheese

1   (8-ounce) bottle Caesar salad dressing

1 Cook the pasta using the package directions; drain well. Combine with the bell peppers, cucumber, olives, artichoke hearts, avocado, chile peppers and green onions in a large bowl. Add the shrimp, pepperoni and cheese; mix gently.

2 Add the salad dressing and toss to coat well. Chill, covered, for 2 to 10 hours. Serve with additional salad dressing if desired.

SERVES 6

Chair ties with tassels can be wrapped around rolled napkins and tied with bows for easy napkin rings.

GREEK TORTELLINI SALAD

2 (9-ounce) packages plain or tricolor fresh cheese tortellini

2 medium red bell peppers, cut into thin strips

1 small red onion, thinly sliced

¼ cup sliced pitted black olives

Mint Vinaigrette

½ cup crumbled feta cheese

1 Cook the pasta using the package directions; drain and cool. Combine with the bell peppers, onion and olives in a large bowl. Pour the Mint Vinaigrette over the salad and toss to coat well.

2 Chill the salad for 4 to 24 hours. Add the cheese at serving time and mix gently.

SERVES 12 TO 14

Mint Vinaigrette

½ cup rice vinegar or white wine vinegar

½ cup olive oil or vegetable oil

3 tablespoons chopped fresh mint, or 2 teaspoons dried

3 tablespoons lemon juice

2 tablespoons dry sherry

1 teaspoon garlic powder

1½ teaspoons seasoned salt

⅛ to ¼ teaspoon crushed red pepper

1 teaspoon black pepper

1 Combine the vinegar, olive oil, mint, lemon juice, sherry, garlic powder, salt, red pepper and black pepper in an airtight jar. Cover the jar and shake to mix well.

2 Store in the refrigerator until needed.

MAKES 1½ CUPS

MEDITERRANEAN SALAD WITH BASIL

2   cups uncooked pasta
     Basil Vinaigrette
6   ounces green beans, trimmed
     salt to taste
2   large tomatoes, sliced
2   cups fresh basil leaves
1   (7-ounce) can oil-pack tuna, drained, flaked
2   hard-cooked eggs, sliced
1   (2-ounce) can anchovy fillets, drained
     capers
     pitted black olives

1 Cook the pasta using the package directions; drain. Combine with a small amount of the Basil Vinaigrette in a bowl and toss lightly.

2 Blanch the beans in lightly salted boiling water in a saucepan for 3 minutes. Refresh under cold water and drain.

3 Arrange the tomatoes in a serving bowl. Drizzle with a small amount of the vinaigrette and top with ¼ of the basil leaves. Layer the beans over the top; drizzle with some of the vinaigrette and top with ⅓ of the remaining basil.

4 Layer the pasta, half the remaining basil, tuna and eggs over the top. Sprinkle with the anchovies, capers and olives. Drizzle with the remaining vinaigrette and top with the remaining basil. Serve immediately.

SERVES 4

Basil Vinaigrette

6   tablespoons extra-virgin olive oil
2   tablespoons white wine vinegar or lemon juice
2   garlic cloves, crushed
½   teaspoon Dijon mustard
2   tablespoons chopped fresh basil
     salt and freshly ground pepper to taste

1 Whisk the olive oil, vinegar, garlic, mustard, basil, salt and pepper in a bowl. Let stand for several minutes.

2 Store in the refrigerator until needed.

MAKES ½ TO ¾ CUP

Pasta Salad del Sol

1 (8-ounce) package seashell pasta

1 (20-ounce) can juice-pack pineapple chunks, drained

2 oranges, peeled, chopped

1 red bell pepper, julienned

1 cup julienned carrots

1 cup frozen peas, thawed

1 cup cashews

1½ cups chopped ham

  Orange Basil Dressing

1 Cook the pasta using the package directions; drain. Combine with the pineapple, oranges, bell pepper, carrots, peas, cashews and ham in a large bowl.

2 Add the Orange Basil Dressing and toss to coat well. Chill, covered, for 1 hour or longer. Reserve the cashews to add at serving time if chilling for longer than 1 hour.

SERVES 6

Orange Basil Dressing

½ cup pineapple juice (from pineapple chunks in salad)

½ cup fresh orange juice

½ cup vegetable oil

1 tablespoon sugar

1 tablespoon grated orange peel

1 tablespoon sweet basil, crumbled

  nutmeg to taste

¼ teaspoon pepper

1 Combine the pineapple juice, orange juice, vegetable oil, sugar, orange peel, basil, nutmeg and pepper in a bowl and whisk until smooth.

2 Store in the refrigerator until needed.

MAKES 1¾ CUPS

TORTELLINI ANTIPASTO SALAD

1   (16-ounce) package fresh or frozen cheese tortellini

4   ounces salami, chopped

4   ounces provolone cheese, cut into strips

1   (11-ounce) can corn kernels, drained

1   (9-ounce) package frozen chopped spinach, thawed, drained

1   (6-ounce) jar marinated artichoke hearts, drained, chopped

1   (6-ounce) can pitted black olives, drained, sliced

1½ cups creamy Italian salad dressing

1   teaspoon Dijon mustard

½   cup grated Parmesan cheese

1   (2-ounce) can sliced pimento (optional)

1   Cook the pasta using the package directions; rinse with cold water and drain. Combine with the salami, provolone cheese, corn, spinach, artichoke hearts and half the olives in a bowl and mix lightly.

2   Blend the salad dressing, mustard and half the Parmesan cheese in a bowl. Add to the salad and toss to mix well. Sprinkle with the remaining olives and Parmesan cheese. Top with the pimento. Chill for 1 to 2 hours.

SERVES 8 TO 10

If you're lighting candles, put out lots of them! Arrange a dozen votives on a table or a mantel. Collect candlesticks of the same material, such as brass, silver, crystal, or wood, and mass them in one area.

PUMPKIN AND PROSCIUTTO LASAGNA

6 leeks, trimmed, rinsed, minced

½ cup unsalted butter

4 cups mashed cooked pumpkin

½ cup dry white wine

  salt and pepper to taste

2 cups walnut pieces

1¼ pounds lasagna noodles, cooked al dente

8 ounces prosciutto, thinly sliced

  Béchamel Sauce

¼ cup torn fresh sage leaves

1½ cups grated Parmesan cheese

1 Sauté the leeks in the butter in a large skillet for 15 minutes or until tender. Stir in the pumpkin and white wine. Cook for 2 minutes, stirring constantly. Remove from the heat and season with salt and pepper.

2 Toast the walnuts on a baking sheet at 350 degrees for 10 to 12 minutes.

3 Arrange ¼ of the noodles in a buttered 10x15-inch baking pan. Layer half the prosciutto and ⅓ of the Béchamel Sauce in the prepared pan. Sprinkle with half the sage. Add ¼ of the noodles, the pumpkin mixture, 1 cup cheese and 1 cup walnuts.

4 Layer with half the remaining noodles, the remaining prosciutto, half the remaining Béchamel Sauce and the remaining sage. Top with the remaining noodles, Béchamel Sauce, walnuts and cheese.

5 Bake at 350 degrees for 50 to 60 minutes or until light brown. To reheat, bake at 350 degrees for 30 to 45 minutes.

SERVES 12

Béchamel Sauce

½ cup unsalted butter

6 tablespoons flour

2 cups chicken broth, at room temperature

2 cups light cream or half-and-half, at room temperature

1 cup grated Parmesan cheese

½ teaspoon nutmeg

  salt and white pepper to taste

3 large eggs, at room temperature, lightly beaten

1 Melt the butter in a saucepan over medium-high heat. Whisk in the flour until smooth. Cook for 1 minute, stirring constantly. Whisk in the chicken broth and then the cream gradually. Cook until thickened and smooth, stirring constantly. Stir in the cheese, nutmeg, salt and white pepper.

2 Stir ½ cup of the hot sauce into the eggs; stir the eggs into the hot sauce. Cook for several minutes, stirring constantly.

MAKES 6½ CUPS

SPAGHETTI PIE

8 ounces uncooked spaghetti, or linguini

2 tablespoons butter

½ cup grated Parmesan cheese

2 eggs, beaten

1 pound ground beef or pork

½ cup chopped onion

¼ cup chopped green bell pepper

1 (8-ounce) can tomatoes, cut up

1 (6-ounce) can tomato paste

1 teaspoon sugar

1 teaspoon dried oregano, crushed

½ teaspoon garlic salt

1 cup cottage cheese

½ cup shredded mozzarella cheese

This freezes well, so make two at once and freeze one for later.

1 Cook the spaghetti using the package directions; drain. Stir in the butter, Parmesan cheese and eggs. Shape into a shell in a buttered 10-inch pie plate.

2 Brown the ground beef with the onion and green pepper in a skillet, stirring until the ground beef is crumbly and cooking until the vegetables are tender; drain. Add the undrained tomatoes, tomato paste, sugar, oregano and garlic salt.

3 Layer the cottage cheese and ground beef mixture in the spaghetti shell. Bake at 350 degrees for 30 minutes. Sprinkle with the mozzarella cheese. Bake for 5 minutes longer.

SERVES 6

When the weather first turns springlike, pull out the cushions for your patio or outdoor furniture to see if they need replacing. Pick an acrylic solid, stripe, or print at Calico Corners that won't fade and you'll have new cushions by the time the weather stays warm for the season.

PORK SAUSAGE AND CHEESE MANICOTTI

14　manicotti shells

2　pounds bulk pork sausage

1　small onion, chopped

2　small tomatoes, chopped

2　cups shredded mild cheese

1　chicken bouillon cube

¼　cup hot water

½　cup white wine

1　cup whipping cream

　　oregano to taste

1　Cook the pasta in boiling water in a saucepan for 8 minutes. Refresh with cold water and drain.

2　Brown the sausage with the onion in a large skillet, stirring until the sausage is crumbly; drain. Stir in the tomatoes and cheese. Spoon the sausage mixture into the pasta shells.

3　Arrange the stuffed shells in a buttered baking dish and cover with foil. Bake at 350 degrees for 20 minutes.

4　Combine the bouillon, hot water and wine in a saucepan. Cook until reduced by ½. Stir in the cream. Simmer until reduced by ½. Season with oregano. Pour over the manicotti.

SERVES 4

RAVIOLI AND CHICKEN WITH PESTO SAUCE

1　pound boneless skinless chicken breasts

2　teaspoons vegetable oil

¾　cup chicken broth

1　(9-ounce) package refrigerated cheese ravioli

3　zucchini, sliced

1　red bell pepper, thinly sliced

¼　cup pesto sauce

　　shredded cheese

1　Cut the chicken into strips. Brown in the heated oil in a 12-inch skillet, turning occasionally. Remove the chicken with a slotted spoon.

2　Add the chicken broth and ravioli to the skillet. Bring to a boil and reduce the heat. Simmer, covered, for 4 minutes or until the pasta is tender.

3　Stir in the zucchini, bell pepper and chicken. Cook for 3 minutes or until the chicken is cooked through, stirring occasionally. Toss with the pesto in a bowl. Sprinkle with cheese.

SERVES 4

LINGUINI WITH TUNA CAPER SAUCE

- **1** tablespoon olive oil
- **1** or 2 garlic cloves, minced
- **1** (16-ounce) can crushed tomatoes
- **1** teaspoon dried oregano, crushed
- **¼** teaspoon red pepper flakes
- **1** (6.5-ounce) can light tuna in water, drained, flaked
- **2** tablespoons capers
- **2** tablespoons minced parsley
- **6** ounces uncooked linguini or spaghetti

This is a very good heart-healthy pasta sauce, made with ingredients that you will probably have on hand. Omit the red pepper flakes for a less spicy sauce.

1 Heat the olive oil in a heavy 10-inch skillet over medium heat for 30 seconds. Add the garlic and sauté for 30 seconds. Stir in the tomatoes, oregano and red pepper flakes.

2 Bring to a boil and reduce the heat to low. Simmer for 7 to 8 minutes or until slightly thickened. Stir in the tuna, capers and parsley. Simmer for 5 minutes longer.

3 Cook the pasta using the package directions. Drain well and place in a heated bowl. Add the tuna sauce and toss to coat well.

SERVES 4

CRAB MEAT PASTA PARMESAN

- **3½** pounds fresh Alaskan King crab legs or frozen crab legs, thawed
- **1** (8-ounce) package fettuccini
- **1** tablespoon butter
- **½** cup part-skim ricotta cheese
- **¼** cup grated Parmesan cheese
- **1** cup cooked peas
- **1** cup chopped tomato
- **2** tablespoons lemon juice
- **2** tablespoons dried basil
- **½** garlic clove, crushed
- salt and pepper to taste

1 Crack the crab legs and remove the meat. Place the crab meat in a microwave-safe dish and cover with plastic wrap. Microwave for 2 minutes.

2 Cook the pasta using the package directions; drain. Add the crab meat, butter, ricotta cheese and Parmesan cheese, peas, tomato, lemon juice, basil and garlic. Season with salt and pepper and toss to mix well.

SERVES 4

BEER-SPIKED SHRIMP AND SPAGHETTI

1   (8-ounce) package spaghetti

2   tablespoons olive oil

2   garlic cloves, minced

8   ounces deveined peeled shrimp

¾   cup beer

1   tablespoon chopped fresh thyme, or
    ½ teaspoon dried thyme leaves

1   Cook the spaghetti using the package directions; keep warm.

2   Heat the olive oil with the garlic in a heavy skillet over medium-high heat. Add the shrimp. Sauté for 3 minutes or until the shrimp are pink. Remove the shrimp to a covered bowl and keep warm.

3   Pour the beer into the skillet. Cook over medium heat for 3 to 4 minutes or until reduced by ½, stirring occasionally. Stir in the thyme.

4   Add the spaghetti, stirring gently. Cook for 1 minute, stirring frequently. Add the shrimp with any accumulated juices; toss lightly.

SERVES 4

BLACKENED SHRIMP WITH PASTA

1   pound deveined peeled fresh shrimp

1   tablespoon olive oil

2   tablespoons blackened seasoning

3   cups sliced fresh mushrooms

1   tablespoon chopped shallots

1   tablespoon butter

⅔   cup dry vermouth or other white wine

½   cup sour cream

1   tablespoon cornstarch

1   cup chicken broth

½   (12-ounce) jar roasted red peppers, drained, cut into strips

1   tablespoon drained capers

12 ounces fettuccini, cooked, drained

1   Mix the shrimp with the olive oil and blackened seasoning in a bowl, coating well. Set aside.

2   Sauté the mushrooms and shallots in the butter in a 10-inch skillet until tender; remove to a bowl with a slotted spoon. Add the shrimp to the skillet and cook over medium-high heat for 2 minutes or until pink. Remove to the bowl with a slotted spoon.

3   Stir the wine into the skillet. Cook for 2 to 3 minutes or until reduced to ¼ cup.

4   Blend the sour cream and cornstarch in a small bowl. Stir in the chicken broth. Add to the skillet. Cook until thickened and bubbly, stirring constantly. Cook for 1 minute longer.

5   Add the shrimp and mushroom mixture, red peppers and capers. Cook until heated through. Serve over the pasta.

SERVES 4

SOUTHWESTERN SEAFOOD LASAGNA

1   cup chopped onion

2   garlic cloves, minced

1   teaspoon margarine

¾   cup 1% milk

¼   cup flour

1   (8-ounce) bottle clam juice or fish bouillon

    chopped green onions to taste

1   jalapeño pepper, seeded, chopped

1   (16-ounce) can no-salt-added cream-style corn

1¼   cups shredded Monterey Jack cheese

1   cup nonfat ricotta cheese

½   cup light cream cheese

¼   cup fresh lime juice

1   pound medium shrimp, peeled, coarsely chopped

8   ounces fresh lump crab meat, drained

9   lasagna noodles, cooked

½   teaspoon ground cumin

¼   teaspoon black pepper

1   Sauté the onion and garlic in the margarine in a saucepan over medium heat for 5 minutes. Whisk the milk gradually into the flour in a bowl. Add to the saucepan with the clam juice. Cook for 5 minutes or until thickened and bubbly, stirring constantly. Add the green onions, jalapeño pepper and corn. Cook for 2 minutes.

2   Process the Monterey Jack cheese, ricotta cheese, cream cheese and lime juice in a food processor until smooth. Combine the shrimp and crab meat in a bowl and toss to mix.

3   Spread ¾ cup of the cream sauce in a 9x13-inch baking dish and arrange 3 noodles in the sauce. Top with half the cheese mixture, half the seafood mixture and ½ cup cream sauce. Add layers of 3 noodles, the remaining cheese mixture, the remaining seafood mixture and the remaining noodles. Top with the remaining cream sauce and sprinkle with cumin and black pepper.

4   Cover with foil sprayed with nonstick cooking spray. Cut ten 1-inch slits in the foil. Bake at 375 degrees for 45 minutes.

SERVES 8

SHRIMP AND PASTA PROVENÇAL

1	(8-ounce) package angel hair pasta
1	tablespoon olive oil
20	large peeled shrimp
	salt and pepper to taste
1	tablespoon olive oil
1	bunch scallions, chopped
8	ounces mushrooms, cut into quarters
2	carrots, peeled, julienned
2	garlic cloves, minced
1/4	cup dry white wine
2	cups Italian-style tomato sauce
1	cup grated Romano cheese
4	ounces feta cheese, cubed

1 Cook the pasta using the package directions; drain and rinse. Toss with 1 tablespoon olive oil and keep warm.

2 Season the shrimp with salt and pepper. Heat 1 tablespoon olive oil in a large sauté pan over high heat until it smokes. Add the shrimp, scallions, mushrooms and carrots. Sauté for 30 seconds. Add the garlic and toss to mix well.

3 Add the wine to the skillet, stirring to deglaze the skillet. Cook for 2½ minutes or until the shrimp are cooked through. Stir in the tomato sauce; remove from the heat.

4 Toss with the Romano cheese and pasta. Cook just until heated through. Top servings with the feta cheese and chopped fresh basil.

SERVES 4

LINGUINI WITH PISTACHIOS

4	ounces uncooked linguini
1	garlic clove, chopped
2	tablespoons thinly sliced shallots
1/4	cup butter
2	tablespoons olive oil
1/2	teaspoon oregano
	pepper to taste
1/4	cup minced parsley
3/4	cup grated Parmesan cheese
1/4	cup chopped pistachios

1 Cook the pasta using the package directions; drain and keep warm.

2 Sauté the garlic and shallots in the heated butter and olive oil in a large sauté pan over medium heat for 1 to 2 minutes. Stir in the oregano and pepper and reduce the heat.

3 Add the pasta and toss gently. Add the parsley, Parmesan cheese and pistachios and toss to mix well. Cook just until heated through. Serve with garlic bread.

SERVES 4

CUCUMBER PENNE

1   small onion, thinly sliced

3   tablespoons butter

3   tablespoons extra-virgin olive oil

4   ounces bacon, crisp-fried, crumbled

8   ounces cucumbers, peeled, seeded, sliced

$2/3$ cup milk

$1/2$ cup cream

$1/2$ chicken bouillon cube

      salt and pepper to taste

1   (16-ounce) package penne

2   tablespoons extra-virgin olive oil

$1/2$ cup shredded Swiss cheese

3   tablespoons chopped parsley

1   Sauté the onion in the heated butter and 3 tablespoons olive oil in a large skillet until light brown. Add the bacon and cucumbers. Sauté for 10 minutes.

2   Bring the milk and cream to a simmer in a saucepan. Stir into the skillet. Add the bouillon cube, salt and pepper. Simmer while the pasta cooks.

3   Cook the pasta using the package directions for 11 minutes or until al dente. Drain and toss with 2 tablespoons olive oil. Combine with the cream sauce and cheese in a bowl and toss to mix well. Sprinkle with the parsley.

SERVES 6

Add a coordinating tableskirt to go with your new cushions for outdoor furniture for al fresco dining or entertaining. If making a square or rectangular shape, you can create a no-sew cover by ironing up a hem and bonding in place with Stitch-Witchery fusible web.

LINGUINI WITH SALSA CRUDA

4   large tomatoes, chopped

16   ounces Montrachet or feta cheese,
       crumbled

1   cup fresh basil strips

3   garlic cloves, minced

1   cup extra-virgin olive oil

2½   teaspoons salt

½   teaspoon freshly ground pepper

6   quarts water

1   tablespoon extra-virgin olive oil

1½   pounds uncooked linguini

This dish works well with almost any type of pasta. The warm pasta brings out the flavor of the uncooked sauce.

1   Combine the tomatoes, cheese, basil, garlic, 1 cup olive oil, ½ teaspoon of the salt and pepper in a large bowl. Let stand for 1 hour or longer to blend the flavors.

2   Bring the water to a boil in a large saucepan. Add 1 tablespoon olive oil, the remaining 2 teaspoons salt and the pasta. Cook for 8 to 10 minutes or until al dente; drain.

3   Add to the tomato mixture and toss to mix well. Serve with grated Parmesan cheese.

SERVES 4 TO 6

SICILIAN FUSILLI WITH BROCCOLI

1   bunch broccoli, chopped

1   (12-ounce) package fusilli

       salt to taste

3   or 4 leeks

½   cup olive oil

4   garlic cloves, minced

8   sun-dried tomatoes in oil, minced

½   cup golden raisins

⅓   cup pine nuts

1   tablespoon (rounded) anchovy paste

       pinch of saffron threads

1   cup grated Romano cheese

       freshly ground pepper to taste

1   Blanch or steam the broccoli just until tender-crisp. Cook the pasta al dente in boiling salted water in a large saucepan; drain, reserving ¾ cup cooking liquid. Keep the broccoli and pasta warm.

2   Mince the white and tender green portions of the leeks. Heat ¼ cup of the olive oil in a large skillet over medium-high heat. Add the leeks and sauté for 10 minutes or until very tender. Add the garlic and sauté for 1 minute longer.

3   Stir in the drained sun-dried tomatoes, raisins, pine nuts, anchovy paste and saffron. Cook over low heat for 5 or 6 minutes or until the flavors blend. Stir in the broccoli and the reserved pasta cooking liquid. Cook just until heated through.

4   Toss with the pasta, the remaining ¼ cup olive oil, Romano cheese and pepper in a serving bowl. Serve immediately.

SERVES 4

PENNE WITH TOMATO VODKA SAUCE

1   small onion, chopped

1   tablespoon butter

1   tablespoon olive oil

1   (28-ounce) can Italian plum tomatoes, drained, seeded, chopped

1   cup whipping cream

¼   cup vodka

¼   teaspoon red pepper flakes, crushed

    salt and black pepper to taste

1   (16-ounce) package penne

    grated Parmesan cheese

    minced chives

1   Sauté the onion in the butter and olive oil in a large heavy saucepan over medium heat for 8 minutes or until translucent. Add the tomatoes and cook for 25 minutes or until the liquid is nearly absorbed.

2   Stir in the cream, vodka and red pepper. Cook for 2 minutes or until thickened to sauce consistency. Season with salt and black pepper.

3   Cook the pasta al dente in boiling water in a large saucepan, stirring occasionally; drain. Combine with the hot tomato vodka sauce in a serving bowl and toss to coat well. Sprinkle with Parmesan cheese and chives.

SERVES 6

Noted textile designer Jack Lenor Larsen taught us a long time ago that a room will be more visually interesting over time if it has a mix of textures— coarse cotton and crisp silk, smooth leather and sumptuous chenille—than if it is done in all very formal textures or all done with informal, casual fabrics.

PASTA WITH ROASTED PEPPERS

1   green bell pepper

1   red bell pepper

1   yellow bell pepper

1   (16-ounce) package pasta

4   garlic cloves

2   tablespoons extra-virgin olive oil

2   tablespoons melted butter

²/₃   cup grated Parmesan cheese

16   to 20 small basil leaves,
      cut into strips

      salt to taste

1   Cut the bell peppers into halves lengthwise. Place cut side down on a baking sheet. Broil until the skin is charred. Place in a nonrecycled paper bag and seal; let stand for 10 minutes. Remove the skins and cut into strips.

2   Cook the pasta using the package directions; keep warm. Sauté the garlic in the olive oil in a saucepan until light brown; remove with a slotted spoon and discard.

3   Combine the pasta, garlic oil, peppers, butter, cheese, basil and salt in a bowl and toss to mix well. Serve immediately.

SERVES 4

TUSCAN PASTA

1   (16-ounce) package ziti

1   tablespoon chopped garlic

2   tablespoons olive oil

2   cups chicken broth

      juice of 2 lemons

1   tablespoon dried parsley

2   tablespoons dried basil

1   tablespoon dried oregano

¹/₃   cup bread crumbs

This low-fat dish has a lemon-herb flavor.

1   Cook the pasta using the package directions; keep warm.

2   Sauté the garlic in the heated olive oil in a saucepan until light brown. Add the chicken broth, lemon juice, parsley, basil and oregano. Simmer for 5 to 10 minutes or until the herbs are rehydrated.

3   Add the bread crumbs and mix well. Add the drained pasta and toss to coat well.

SERVES 4 TO 6

PEPPERCORN PASTA SAUCE

4	pounds tomatoes
2	(6-ounce) jars marinated artichoke hearts
½	cup extra-virgin olive oil
2	cups coarsely chopped yellow onions
4	garlic cloves, minced
¼	cup dried basil
½	tablespoon dried oregano
½	cup minced Italian parsley
1	dried small red pepper, crushed
1½ to 3	tablespoons whole black peppercorns
1	teaspoon salt
¼	cup grated Romano cheese

Great over mushroom tortellini, this recipe makes enough sauce for three pounds of pasta. It also can be mixed with the pasta, cooled, and served at room temperature.

1 Scald the tomatoes several at a time in boiling water for 10 seconds; remove with a slotted spoon and plunge into ice water. Drain and remove the skins. Cut crosswise into halves, seed and chop coarsely. Drain the artichokes, reserving the marinade. Cut the artichokes into halves.

2 Heat the olive oil in a large saucepan over medium heat. Add the onions, garlic, basil, oregano, parsley and red pepper and sauté for 5 minutes.

3 Crush the peppercorns using a mortar and pestle or coffee grinder. Add the crushed peppercorns, tomatoes and salt to the saucepan. Simmer over medium heat for 1 hour. Stir in the desired amount of reserved artichoke marinade and simmer for 30 minutes longer, stirring frequently. Add the artichokes and simmer for 20 minutes or until of the desired consistency. Stir in the cheese and adjust the seasoning. Serve over cooked pasta.

MAKES ENOUGH FOR 3 POUNDS OF PASTA

According to British author and designer Mary Gilliat, "The best thing about American design is the use of color—the clear, stronger colors used here because of the difference in the quality of light."

DESSERTS · CANDY · COOKIES

Berry Cloud with Brandied Cream

6   large egg whites, at room temperature

1   teaspoon vanilla extract

1½ cups sugar

½   cup finely ground hazelnuts

1½ cups whipping cream

2   tablespoons confectioners' sugar

2   teaspoons brandy

2   cups fresh whole raspberries, blueberries, blackberries and/or small strawberries

    mint sprigs

A great light dessert perfect with summer berries.

1   Line baking sheets with foil and trace three 7-inch circles on the foil.

2   Combine the egg whites and vanilla in a large mixer bowl and beat at medium speed until soft peaks form. Add the sugar 1 tablespoon at a time, beating constantly at high speed until stiff peaks form and the sugar is dissolved. Fold in the hazelnuts gently.

3   Spoon the meringue onto the circles and spread evenly to the edges. Bake at 300 degrees for 45 minutes, rotating the baking sheets after 20 minutes to ensure even browning. Turn off the oven and let the meringues stand in the oven for 1 hour; do not open the oven.

4   Combine the whipping cream, confectioners' sugar and brandy in a chilled mixer bowl. Beat with chilled beaters until soft peaks form.

5   Spread a small amount of the whipped cream on a cake stand. Layer 1 meringue on the stand. Spoon ⅓ of the remaining whipped cream on the meringue, spreading almost to the edge. Top with ⅓ of the berries. Repeat the layers twice.

6   Chill for 3 hours or longer. Slice to serve. Garnish with mint sprigs and additional berries.

SERVES 6

Float furnishings. When furniture is arranged around the edges of a room, it creates an awkward ballroom feel or waiting-room look. Pull furniture into groupings that invite conversation.

BLUEBERRY CHEESECAKE

1   **pound cottage cheese**

1   **pound cream cheese, softened**

1½ **cups sugar**

4   **large eggs**

3   **tablespoons cornstarch**

3   **tablespoons flour**

5   **teaspoons lemon juice**

1   **tablespoon vanilla extract**

¼   **cup melted butter, cooled**

2   **cups sour cream**

     Blueberry Sauce

1 Process the cottage cheese in batches in a food processor or blender until smooth. Combine with the cream cheese in a mixer bowl and beat until smooth. Beat in the sugar gradually.

2 Beat the eggs in a medium bowl until thick and pale yellow. Add to the cheese mixture and beat until smooth. Add the cornstarch, flour, lemon juice, vanilla, butter and sour cream and mix well.

3 Spoon into a buttered 10-inch springform pan. Bake at 325 degrees for 1 hour. Turn off the oven and let the cheesecake stand in the oven for 2 hours; do not open the oven door.

4 Cool completely on a wire rack. Chill, covered, for 8 hours or longer. Place on a serving plate and remove the side of the pan. Serve with Blueberry Sauce.

SERVES 12

Blueberry Sauce

⅓   **cup sugar**

1½ **tablespoons flour**

¼   **teaspoon salt**

¾   **cup minus 1 tablespoon hot water**

1   **tablespoon lemon juice**

1   **cup fresh blueberries**

2   **to 4 tablespoons dark rum**

2   **teaspoons unsalted butter, softened**

1 Mix the sugar, flour and salt in a saucepan. Add the hot water gradually, stirring constantly. Stir in the lemon juice. Bring to a boil, stirring constantly. Add the blueberries. Simmer for 2 to 5 minutes or until thickened; remove from the heat.

2 Add the rum and butter and beat until smooth. Let stand until cooled to room temperature.

MAKES 2¼ CUPS

GERMAN CHOCOLATE CHEESECAKE

1   (8.5-ounce) package chocolate
      wafers, crushed

½   cup flaked coconut

½   cup melted butter or margarine

¾   cup sugar

24   ounces cream cheese, softened

3   eggs

8   ounces semisweet chocolate, melted

2   tablespoons baking cocoa

2   tablespoons rum or brandy

1   teaspoon vanilla extract

16   ounces sour cream

¼   cup flour, sifted

      Coconut Pecan Topping

      flaked coconut

      pecan halves

1   Combine the cookie crumbs, ½ cup coconut and butter in a medium bowl and mix well. Press over the bottom and up the side of a 9-inch springform pan. Chill in the refrigerator.

2   Beat the sugar and cream cheese at high speed in a mixer bowl until fluffy. Beat in the eggs 1 at a time. Stir in the chocolate, baking cocoa, rum and vanilla. Beat in the sour cream. Fold in the flour. Spoon into the prepared springform pan.

3   Bake at 325 degrees for 1 hour or until the edge is set but the center is still soft. Turn off the oven and let the cheesecake stand in the oven for 1 hour; do not open the oven door.

4   Cool in the pan on a wire rack; the top may crack. Chill in the refrigerator until firm. Place on a serving plate and remove the side of the pan. Spread the Coconut Pecan Topping over the cheesecake. Top with a circle of coconut and pecans halves. Cut into thin slices to serve.

SERVES 12

Coconut Pecan Topping

⅔   cup evaporated milk

⅔   cup sugar

2   egg yolks, slightly beaten

½   cup butter

1   teaspoon vanilla extract

¾   cup flaked coconut

½   cup chopped pecans

1   Combine the evaporated milk, sugar, egg yolks, butter and vanilla in a small saucepan and mix well. Cook over medium heat for 12 minutes or until heated through, stirring constantly.

2   Stir in the coconut and pecans. Cool until of spreading consistency.

MAKES 3¼ CUPS

CHOCOLATE MOUSSE DESSERT

1   cup chocolate wafer crumbs

¼   cup melted butter or margarine

3   (12-ounce) packages semisweet
     chocolate chips

¾   cup butter or margarine

5   egg yolks

2   teaspoons instant coffee granules

⅓   cup orange liqueur

2   cups whipping cream

5   egg whites

¼   cup confectioners' sugar
     Chocolate Glaze

Use an equivalent amount of commercial egg substitute if you prefer not to use raw eggs.

1   Combine the cookie crumbs and ¼ cup butter in a bowl and mix well. Press over the bottom of a 10-inch springform pan. Chill in the refrigerator.

2   Melt the chocolate chips and ¾ cup butter in a 4-quart saucepan, stirring constantly to mix well; remove from the heat.

3   Whisk the egg yolks and coffee granules in a medium bowl until smooth. Blend into the chocolate mixture. Stir in the liqueur.

4   Beat the whipping cream at medium speed in a mixer bowl until soft peaks forms. Fold into the chocolate mixture ½ at a time.

5   Beat the eggs whites in a mixer bowl until foamy. Add the confectioners' sugar and beat until stiff peaks form. Fold into the chocolate mixture ½ at a time. Spoon into the prepared springform pan. Chill, covered, for 8 hours or longer.

6   Place the mousse on a wire rack over waxed paper and remove the side. Spoon the Chocolate Glaze over the mousse. Let stand until set. Place on a serving plate.

SERVES 12

Chocolate Glaze

1½ cups semisweet chocolate chips

3   tablespoons orange liqueur

3   tablespoons milk

1   teaspoon instant coffee granules

2   tablespoons confectioners' sugar

1   Combine the chocolate chips, liqueur, milk, coffee granules and confectioners' sugar in a saucepan.

2   Cook over low heat until the chocolate chips melt, stirring to blend well. Let stand until cool.

MAKES 2 CUPS

CRANBERRY APPLE CRISP

4	Granny Smith apples, peeled, thinly sliced
3	cups cranberries
½	cup sugar
1	teaspoon cinnamon
¼	cup flour
2	tablespoons brown sugar
¾	cup rolled oats
3	tablespoons melted butter or margarine

Easy to make and great for a snack as well as dessert.

1 Combine the apples, cranberries, sugar, cinnamon and 1 tablespoon of the flour in a bowl; toss to mix well. Spoon into a shallow 6-cup baking dish sprayed with nonstick cooking spray.

2 Mix the remaining flour with the brown sugar and oats in the same bowl. Add the melted butter and mix until crumbly. Sprinkle over the apples.

3 Bake at 375 degrees for 40 minutes or until light brown. Let stand for 10 minutes before serving.

SERVES 6

FLAN

½	cup sugar
5	eggs
1	(14-ounce) can sweetened condensed milk
1	(12-ounce) can evaporated milk
1¾	cups milk
1	teaspoon vanilla extract

This can be made with all fat-free milk.

1 Sprinkle the sugar in a heavy saucepan. Cook over medium heat until the sugar melts and becomes caramel colored. Pour into a 6-cup baking dish, swirling to coat the bottom well. Cool completely.

2 Combine the eggs, sweetened milk, evaporated milk, milk and vanilla in a blender container and process until smooth. Pour into the prepared baking dish. Set the dish in a large baking pan and add 1 inch hot water.

3 Bake at 350 degrees for 1 hour or until a knife inserted in the flan comes out clean. Cool on a wire rack. Invert onto a serving plate. Serve with fresh berries and whipped cream.

SERVES 6

GINGERBREAD

1 cup dark molasses

1 cup (scant) nonfat sour cream

2 tablespoons melted butter

¼ cup packed brown sugar

1 large egg

1 teaspoon baking soda

1 tablespoon ground ginger

1 teaspoon salt

2 cups flour

½ cup chopped candied ginger

   Citrus Sauce

1 Combine the molasses, sour cream, butter, brown sugar, egg, baking soda, ground ginger and salt in a mixer bowl and beat until smooth. Add the flour and mix just until blended. Stir in the candied ginger.

2 Spoon into a greased 8-inch baking pan. Bake at 350 degrees for 50 to 60 minutes or until a wooden pick inserted in the center comes out clean. Serve with warm Citrus Sauce.

SERVES 6

Citrus Sauce

½ cup sugar

1 tablespoon cornstarch

1 cup water

1 tablespoon butter

3 tablespoons fresh lemon juice

1½ teaspoons grated lemon peel

   sections of 2 navel oranges, about 1 cup

1 Mix the sugar and cornstarch in a small saucepan. Stir in the water. Bring to a boil and boil for 1 minute or until thickened and clear, stirring constantly; remove from the heat.

2 Stir in the butter, lemon juice, lemon peel and oranges.

MAKES 2½ CUPS

Gooey Baked Alaska

1   package brownie mix

2   quarts coffee, strawberry, cinnamon or peppermint ice cream, softened

5   egg whites

¾   cup sugar

1   Prepare and bake the brownie mix using the package directions for a round 8-inch baking pan. Cool to room temperature.

2   Line a round-bottom 7- to 8-inch bowl with waxed paper; do not use plastic wrap. Spoon the ice cream into the bowl. Freeze until firm.

3   Beat the egg whites at high speed in a mixer bowl until foamy. Add the sugar gradually, beating constantly until stiff peaks form.

4   Invert the brownie layer onto a baking sheet. Invert the ice cream onto the brownie and remove the waxed paper. Spread with the meringue. Freeze until serving time.

5   Preheat the broiler to 500 degrees. Place the Alaska on the lowest oven rack and broil for 30 seconds to 2 minutes or just until light brown. Remove to a serving plate. Let stand for 10 minutes.

SERVES 8 TO 10

Ice Cream with Grand Marnier Sauce

4   cups whipping cream

2   cups sugar

1   cup lemon juice

½   cup whipping cream

8   ounces semisweet chocolate, coarsely chopped

¼   cup Grand Marnier

     mint sprigs or candied lemon

The sauce can also be used with a good commercial coffee ice cream.

1   Beat 4 cups whipping cream with the sugar in a mixer bowl just until well mixed. Stir in the lemon juice; the mixture will appear curdled. Place in the ice cream freezer container and freeze using the manufacturer's instructions.

2   Combine ½ cup whipping cream with the chocolate in a double boiler. Cook over simmering water until the chocolate melts, stirring to blend well. Stir in the Grand Marnier. Cool to room temperature.

3   Spoon a thin layer of the Grand Marnier sauce onto 12 serving plates, reheating slightly over simmering water if necessary to spread evenly. Scoop the ice cream into the center of the plates. Garnish with mint sprigs or candied lemon. Serve immediately.

SERVES 12

Lemon Soufflé with Strawberry Sauce

1   envelope unflavored gelatin

½   cup cold water

4   egg yolks

     juice of 2 lemons

½   cup sugar

½   teaspoon salt

     grated peel of 1 lemon

4   egg whites

½   cup sugar

1   cup whipping cream, whipped

     Strawberry Sauce

A superb ending to a spring or summer dinner—and it can all be made ahead of time. The soufflé is unsinkable.

1   Sprinkle the gelatin over the cold water and let stand until softened.

2   Combine the egg yolks, lemon juice, ½ cup sugar and salt in a double boiler. Cook over simmering water until thickened and smooth, stirring constantly with a wooden spoon; remove from the heat. Add the gelatin, stirring until dissolved. Add the lemon peel. Cool to room temperature.

3   Beat the egg whites in a mixer bowl until soft peaks form. Add ½ cup sugar gradually, beating constantly until stiff shiny peaks form.

4   Whisk ⅓ of the egg whites into the lemon mixture. Fold in the remaining egg whites gently. Fold in the whipped cream gently.

5   Spoon into a soufflé dish. Cover with plastic wrap and chill for 2 hours or until firm. Spoon into serving dishes and top with Strawberry Sauce.

SERVES 8

Strawberry Sauce

1   quart fresh strawberries, hulled

½   to ¾ cup sugar or superfine sugar

2   to 3 tablespoons kirsch, Cognac or lemon juice

1   Purée the strawberries in a blender or food processor, adding the sugar gradually and processing constantly until the sugar dissolves and the mixture is thick. Add the kirsch. Chill until serving time.

2   You may use thawed frozen whole strawberries or substitute raspberries for the strawberries. You may also prepare the sauce by beating for 10 minutes with an electric mixer.

MAKES 3 CUPS

LINZERTORTE

½ cup butter, softened

1 cup sugar

1 egg

1 cup flour

1 teaspoon baking powder

1 teaspoon cinnamon

1 cup ground hazelnuts

  raspberry preserves

1 Cream the butter and sugar in a mixer bowl until light and fluffy. Beat in the egg. Mix the flour, baking powder and cinnamon together. Add to the creamed mixture and mix well. Add the hazelnuts and mix or knead until well mixed. Chill for 30 minutes.

2 Divide the dough into ⅓ and ⅔ portions. Press the larger portion into a greased and floured pie plate. Spread with preserves. Divide the smaller portion of dough into balls and roll into thin ropes. Arrange in a crisscross pattern across the top.

3 Bake at 325 degrees for 30 to 40 minutes or just until golden brown. Cool on a wire rack.

SERVES 8

PEACH COBBLER

6 cups sliced peeled peaches

1 cup sugar

  grated zest of 1 lemon

  juice of ½ lemon

¼ teaspoon almond extract

1½ cups flour

1 tablespoon baking powder

½ teaspoon salt

⅓ cup shortening

1 egg, slightly beaten

¼ cup milk

1 cup whipping cream, chilled

3 tablespoons peach brandy

A delicious ending to a summer dinner party.

1 Toss the peaches with ⅔ cup of the sugar, lemon zest, lemon juice and almond extract in a bowl. Spoon into a buttered 2-quart baking dish. Bake at 400 degrees for 20 minutes.

2 Sift the flour, 1 tablespoon sugar, baking powder and salt into a bowl. Cut in the shortening until the mixture resembles fine crumbs. Add the egg and milk and mix just until moistened.

3 Drop by spoonfuls over the peaches; sprinkle with the remaining sugar. Bake for 15 to 20 minutes or until the topping is golden brown.

4 Beat the cream in a mixer bowl until soft peaks form. Stir in the peach brandy. Serve with the warm cobbler.

SERVES 4 TO 6

PLUM KUCHEN

2	cups sifted flour
1	teaspoon baking powder
½	teaspoon salt
1½	cups sugar
½	cup chilled butter
½	cup milk
1	egg, beaten
	fresh Italian plums, cut into halves
1	teaspoon cinnamon
1	egg, beaten

A favorite recipe from a favorite Italian grandmother.

1 Sift the flour, baking powder, salt and 1 cup of the sugar into a bowl. Add the butter and mix to the consistency of coarse meal with a pastry blender. Add the milk and 1 egg all at once and mix just until moistened. Spread in a buttered baking pan.

2 Arrange the plums cut side up in the prepared pan. Sprinkle with the remaining ½ cup sugar and cinnamon. Brush with 1 beaten egg. Bake at 350 degrees for 30 minutes.

SERVES 6

BREAD PUDDING WITH APPLES

2	tablespoons butter
1½	pounds Golden Delicious apples, peeled, thinly sliced, about 4 cups
¼	cup sugar
¼	cup raisins or currants
¼	cup Calvados or applejack (optional)
10	to 20 (½-inch) slices dried French bread
4	egg yolks
2	eggs
1	cup sugar
1	cup whipping cream
3	cups milk
1	teaspoon vanilla extract

For a heart-healthy version, substitute one two-egg-equivalent package of egg substitute plus one whole egg and one egg white for the eggs and egg yolks and evaporated milk for the heavy cream.

1 Heat the butter in a heavy skillet and add the apple slices. Sprinkle with ¼ cup sugar and add the raisins. Drizzle with the brandy and ignite; remove from the heat when the flames subside.

2 Arrange the bread in a single overlapping layer in an oval 8x14-inch or a rectangular 9x13-inch baking dish; do not crowd the bread. Spoon the apple mixture over the bread.

3 Combine the egg yolks, eggs, 1 cup sugar, cream, milk and vanilla in a mixer bowl and mix until smooth. Pour over the apples.

4 Place in a large baking pan filled halfway with boiling water. Bake at 400 degrees for 35 to 40 minutes or until the top is golden brown. Let stand until lukewarm; sift confectioners' sugar over the top to serve.

SERVES 6 TO 8

APPLES IN BASKETS

1	package frozen puff pastry, thawed
1	cup apple jam
1	cup crushed amaretti cookies
4	Golden Delicious apples
	sugar to taste
	cinnamon to taste
1	egg, beaten

You may substitute a mixture of butter, brown sugar, raisins, walnuts, cinnamon, and nutmeg for the apple jam in this recipe.

1 Roll the pastry ¼ inch thick on a floured surface. Cut into 8 squares. Spread each square with 2 tablespoons jam and sprinkle with cookie crumbs.

2 Peel the apples and cut into halves, discarding the cores. Cut into slices, retaining the shape of the apple. Place 1 apple half on each square. Sprinkle with sugar and cinnamon.

3 Brush the corners of the pastry with the egg. Pull up the corners to cover the apple and press to seal. Decorate with leaf shapes cut from leftover pastry; attach with a whole clove. Brush with the egg and sprinkle with sugar. Place in an ungreased baking dish. Bake at 375 degrees for 15 minutes or until the pastry is golden brown and the apples are tender. Serve with vanilla ice cream if desired.

SERVES 8

ALMOND TOFFEE

2	cups sugar
1	pound butter
1	cup semisweet chocolate chips
1	(2- to 3-ounce) package almonds, finely chopped

1 Combine the sugar and butter in an electric skillet. Set the temperature at the lowest setting. Cook until the light goes out to indicate that the temperature has been reached, stirring constantly. Continue to increase the temperature and cook in the same manner until the temperature reaches 375 degrees and the mixture is golden brown.

2 Pour into an ungreased 10x15-inch pan. Sprinkle with the chocolate chips and let stand until softened. Spread the softened chocolate evenly over the top. Sprinkle with the almonds.

3 Chill in the refrigerator. Break into pieces.

SERVES 10

CANDY

FOOLPROOF CHOCOLATE FUDGE

1   (14-ounce) can sweetened
    condensed milk

18 ounces semisweet chocolate chips

¹⁄₈ teaspoon salt

¹⁄₂ to 2 cups pecans halves

1¹⁄₂ teaspoons vanilla, brandy or
    rum extract

1   Combine the condensed milk, chocolate chips and salt in a heavy saucepan. Cook over low heat for 30 minutes or until the chocolate chips melt; remove from the heat. Stir in the pecans and vanilla.

2   Pour into a square 8- or 9-inch dish lined with foil or waxed paper. Chill for 2 hours or until firm. Invert onto a cutting board and remove the foil or waxed paper. Cut into squares. Store loosely covered at room temperature.

3   You may substitute milk chocolate chips for some of the semisweet chips.

MAKES 3 TO 3¹⁄₂ POUNDS

PEANUT BUTTER BALLS

2   cups graham cracker crumbs

1   cup peanut butter

¹⁄₂ cup melted margarine

¹⁄₂ (1-pound) package confectioners'
    sugar

10 ounces semisweet chocolate chips

¹⁄₄ block paraffin

1   Combine the graham cracker crumbs, peanut butter, margarine and confectioners' sugar in a bowl and mix well. Shape into ³⁄₄-inch balls. Chill in the refrigerator.

2   Melt the chocolate chips with the paraffin in a double boiler, stirring to mix well. Use a wooden pick to dip the peanut butter balls into the chocolate mixture; place on waxed paper and let stand until firm.

MAKES 4 DOZEN

BIRD'S NEST COOKIES

½   cup butter, softened

¼   cup packed brown sugar

1   egg yolk

1⅓   cups flour

     salt to taste

1   egg white, slightly beaten

1   pound unroasted walnuts, very finely chopped

½   cup raspberry jam

1   Combine the butter, brown sugar and egg yolk in a mixer bowl and beat until light and smooth. Add the flour and salt and mix to form a firm dough. Shape into small balls. Dip into the egg white and roll in the walnuts, coating well.

2   Place on a cookie sheet and press an indentation in the center of each cookie. Bake at 325 degrees for 5 minutes. Press the indentation again. Bake for 10 minutes longer or until light brown. Fill the indentations with the jam. Cool on a wire rack.

MAKES 3 DOZEN

BISCOTTI

1   cup vegetable oil

4   large eggs

1   cup sugar

1   teaspoon almond extract

4   cups flour

2   teaspoons baking powder

1   cup ground almonds or hazelnuts (optional)

1   Combine the oil, eggs, sugar and almond extract in a mixer bowl and beat until thick and pale yellow. Mix the flour and baking powder together. Add the flour mixture and almonds to the oil mixture and mix well.

2   Shape into 6 loaves 12 inches long and 1 inch in height with floured hands; place on 2 ungreased cookie sheets. Bake at 350 degrees for 30 minutes. Cool on wire racks for several minutes.

3   Slice diagonally ½ inch thick. Place cut side down on cookie sheets. Bake for 15 minutes or until golden brown. Remove to wire racks to cool.

4   For variety, sprinkle the tops of the loaves with cinnamon and sugar, add baking cocoa to the dry ingredients or add milk chocolate or white chocolate chips. You may dip the cookies into chocolate, pipe chocolate onto the tops or spread with Nutella, which is a hazelnut butter and cocoa spread.

MAKES 12 DOZEN

BROWNIE DECADENCE

½   **cup margarine**

1½   **cups sugar**

3   **eggs**

2   **teaspoons vanilla extract**

¾   **cup baking cocoa**

1   **cup flour**

½   **teaspoon salt**

     Pecan Praline Topping

2   **ounces semisweet chocolate, melted**

1   Place the margarine in a microwave-safe mixing bowl. Microwave on High until melted. Add the sugar and mix well. Stir in the eggs 1 at a time. Mix in the vanilla, baking cocoa, flour and salt.

2   Spoon into a greased round 10-inch baking pan. Bake at 350 degrees for 20 minutes. Cool on a wire rack. Remove to a serving plate.

3   Spoon the Pecan Praline Topping over the brownie layer. Chill for 8 hours or longer. Cut into 16 to 20 wedges. Pipe the chocolate over each wedge.

SERVES 16 TO 20

Pecan Praline Topping

1   **cup sugar**

1   **cup minus 2 tablespoons whipping cream**

⅔   **cup butter**

1   **cup toasted chopped pecans**

1   Sprinkle the sugar into a heavy saucepan. Cook over medium heat until the sugar melts and is caramel-colored, stirring constantly. Stir in the whipping cream carefully; the mixture will boil up. Stir in the butter 1 tablespoon at a time. Mix in the pecans.

2   Do not substitute for the butter in this recipe.

MAKES 3 CUPS

CHEESECAKE BARS

- ⅓ cup butter, softened
- ⅓ cup packed brown sugar
- 1 cup flour
- ½ cup (heaping) chopped pecans or walnuts
- 8 ounces cream cheese
- ¼ cup sugar
- 1 egg
- 2 tablespoons milk
- 1 tablespoon lemon juice
- ½ teaspoon vanilla extract

If you eat one bar, you won't be able to stop. You might even hide them in the refrigerator and eat them all yourself!

1 Cream the butter and brown sugar in a small mixer bowl until light and fluffy. Add the flour and pecans and mix until crumbly. Reserve 1 cup of the crumb mixture for the topping.

2 Press the remaining crumb mixture over the bottom of an 8x8-inch baking pan. Bake at 350 degrees for 12 minutes or until light brown.

3 Beat the cream cheese and sugar in a mixer bowl until smooth. Add the egg, milk, lemon juice and vanilla and mix well. Spread over the baked layer; sprinkle with the reserved crumb mixture.

4 Bake for 25 minutes. Cool on a wire rack and cut into 2-inch bars. Store in the refrigerator.

MAKES 32 BARS

CHOCOLATE CHIP COOKIES

- ½ cup rolled oats
- 2 cups self-rising flour
- 1 (3-ounce) package vanilla instant pudding mix
- ¾ cup sugar
- ¾ cup packed dark brown sugar
- 1 cup butter, softened, cut into chunks
- 2 eggs
- 1 teaspoon vanilla extract
- 12 ounces semisweet chocolate chips

1 Pulse the oats in the food processor until finely ground. Add the flour and pudding mix and pulse to mix well. Remove to a large bowl.

2 Pulse the sugar and brown sugar in the food processor to mix well; set aside. Process the butter in the food processor until creamy. Add the sugar mixture and process until fluffy. Add the eggs and vanilla and pulse until smooth. Stir into the oat mixture. Stir in the chocolate chips.

3 Drop by spoonfuls onto a large cookie sheet. Bake at 375 degrees for 10 minutes; do not overbake. Cool on the cookie sheet for several minutes; remove to a wire rack to cool completely.

MAKES 3 TO 4 DOZEN

GRANDMOTHER'S GINGER COOKIES

¾ cup shortening

1 cup sugar

1 egg

¼ cup molasses

2 cups sifted flour

2 teaspoons baking soda

1 teaspoon ginger

1 teaspoon cinnamon

½ teaspoon salt

sugar

1 Cream the shortening and 1 cup sugar in a mixer bowl until light and fluffy. Beat in the egg and molasses. Sift the flour, baking soda, ginger, cinnamon and salt together twice. Return to the sifter and sift over the creamed mixture; mix well.

2 Shape into 1-inch balls; roll in additional sugar. Place 2 inches apart on an ungreased cookie sheet. Bake at 350 degrees for 12 to 15 minutes or until the tops are slightly puffed and crackly. Cool on the cookie sheet for several minutes; remove to a wire rack to cool completely.

MAKES 4 DOZEN

GOOEY BUTTER SQUARES

1 (2-layer) package yellow cake mix

½ cup butter

1 egg

1 cup chopped pecans

8 ounces cream cheese, softened

2 eggs

1 (1-pound) package confectioners' sugar

1 Combine the cake mix, butter, egg and pecans in a bowl and mix until crumbly. Press over the bottom of a 9x13-inch baking pan. Beat the cream cheese in a mixer bowl until fluffy. Add the eggs and confectioners' sugar gradually and mix well.

2 Pour into the prepared baking pan. Bake at 350 degrees for 45 to 55 minutes or until light brown. Cool on a wire rack. Cut into squares. Store for 48 hours before serving to improve the flavor.

MAKES 2 DOZEN

HONEY CAKES

¾ **cup unblanched almonds**

2 **ounces candied orange peel**

2 **ounces candied lemon peel**

2 **ounces candied citron (optional)**

4 **pieces crystallized ginger (optional)**

3 **cups sifted flour**

¼ **teaspoon baking soda**

½ **teaspoon cinnamon**

½ **teaspoon allspice**

½ **teaspoon nutmeg**

½ **teaspoon ground cloves**

2 **eggs**

1 **cup sugar**

½ **cup honey**

⅓ **cup confectioners' sugar**

1 **tablespoon water**

1 **teaspoon lemon juice**

1 Combine the almonds, orange peel, lemon peel, citron and crystallized ginger in a food processor container and process until finely chopped; set aside.

2 Sift the flour, baking soda, cinnamon, allspice, nutmeg and cloves together. Beat the eggs and sugar in a mixer bowl until thick and pale yellow. Beat in the honey. Fold in the dry ingredients gradually. Stir in the fruit mixture.

3 Spoon the mixture into a greased 10x15-inch baking pan, spreading evenly to the corners. Bake at 350 degrees for 25 to 30 minutes or until a wooden pick inserted in the center comes out clean. Cool slightly on a wire rack.

4 Combine the confectioners' sugar, water and lemon juice in a bowl and mix until smooth. Spread over the baked layer. Cut into bars.

MAKES 3 DOZEN

Upholster an ottoman or a slipper chair in terry cloth for the master bath; it's the perfect spot to trim nails, splash on lotions, or drape a robe.

LEMON COCONUT COOKIES

1   cup butter, softened
½   cup sugar
2   cups flour
1   teaspoon baking powder
½   teaspoon salt
1½ tablespoons grated lemon peel
1   teaspoon vanilla extract
½   teaspoon lemon extract
1   cup toasted flaked coconut

1   Cream the butter and sugar in a mixer bowl until light and fluffy. Add the flour, baking powder, salt, lemon peel and flavorings; mix well. Mix in the coconut. Shape into 2 logs and wrap in waxed paper. Chill for 8 hours or longer.

2   Cut into ¼-inch slices. Arrange on a cookie sheet. Bake at 300 degrees for 25 to 30 minutes or until golden brown. Cool on the cookie sheet for several minutes. Remove to a wire rack to cool completely.

MAKES 4 TO 5 DOZEN

LEMON SUPREMES

½   cup unsalted butter, softened
1   cup flour
¼   cup confectioners' sugar
2   tablespoons fresh lemon juice
    grated peel of 1 lemon
2   large eggs, slightly beaten
½   teaspoon baking powder
1   tablespoon flour
1   cup sugar
    confectioners' sugar

1   Cream the butter, 1 cup flour and ¼ cup confectioners' sugar in a mixer bowl until light and fluffy. Press over the bottom of a 9x9-inch baking pan. Bake at 350 degrees for 15 minutes.

2   Whisk the lemon juice, lemon peel, eggs, baking powder, 1 tablespoon flour and sugar in a bowl. Pour over the baked layer.

3   Bake for 25 minutes longer. Cool completely in the pan on a wire rack. Sprinkle with confectioners' sugar and cut into squares.

MAKES 16 SQUARES

SMASHED OATMEAL COOKIES

1	cup shortening
1	cup sugar
½	cup packed brown sugar
1	egg, beaten
1½	cups flour
1	teaspoon baking soda
1	teaspoon cinnamon
1½	cups quick-cooking oats
¾	cup finely chopped walnuts or pecans
1	teaspoon vanilla extract
	sugar

Chilling the cookie dough, shaping it into balls, and pressing with a buttered and sugared glass bottom will work for nearly any cookie recipe that calls for rolling and cutting with a cookie cutter, and it's a lot easier.

1 Cream the shortening, sugar and brown sugar in a mixer bowl until light and fluffy. Beat in the egg. Sift in the flour, baking soda and cinnamon. Add the oats, walnuts and vanilla and mix well.

2 Chill for 1 hour. Shape into 1-inch balls and place on a greased cookie sheet. Press with the bottom of a glass that has been buttered and dipped in sugar, redipping the glass in the sugar after each cookie press.

3 Bake at 350 degrees for 10 minutes. Cool on the cookie sheet for several minutes. Remove to a wire rack to cool completely.

MAKES 3 DOZEN

PEANUT BUTTER COOKIES

½	cup margarine, softened
½	cup sugar
½	cup packed light brown sugar
1	egg
1	cup peanut butter
1	to 1½ cups sifted flour
½	teaspoon baking soda
½	teaspoon vanilla extract
1	(7-ounce) chocolate bar, chopped
1½	cups chopped pecans

1 Cream the margarine, sugar and brown sugar in a mixer bowl until light and fluffy. Beat in the egg and peanut butter. Add the flour, baking soda and vanilla and mix well. Mix in the chocolate and pecans.

2 Shape into small balls and place on a cookie sheet. Press with a fork to flatten. Bake at 375 degrees for 10 to 12 minutes or until light brown. Cool on the cookie sheet for several minutes. Remove to a wire rack to cool completely.

MAKES 5 DOZEN

PECAN SANDIES

1   **cup butter, softened**
¼   **cup confectioners' sugar**
2   **teaspoons vanilla extract**
1   **tablespoon water**
2   **cups sifted flour**
1   **cup chopped pecans**

Great for the holidays!

1   Cream the butter in a large mixer bowl until light. Add the confectioners' sugar and beat until fluffy. Add the vanilla, water and flour and mix well. Mix in the pecans.

2   Shape into balls or small logs and place on ungreased cookie sheets. Bake at 300 degrees for 20 minutes. Roll warm cookies in additional confectioners' sugar. Cool on a wire rack and roll again in confectioners' sugar

MAKES 3 DOZEN

PINEAPPLE DROP COOKIES

1   **cup shortening**
1   **cup sugar**
1   **cup packed brown sugar**
½   **teaspoon salt**
1   **teaspoon vanilla extract**
2   **eggs, slightly beaten**
4   **cups flour**
2   **teaspoons baking powder**
½   **teaspoon baking soda**
1   **cup slightly drained crushed pineapple**
    nuts and shredded coconut to taste

1   Combine the shortening, sugar, brown sugar, salt, vanilla and eggs in a mixer bowl and mix until smooth. Sift in the flour, baking powder and baking soda and mix well. Mix in the pineapple, nuts and coconut.

2   Drop by spoonfuls onto greased cookie sheets. Bake at 350 to 375 degrees for 12 to 15 minutes or until golden brown. Cool on the cookie sheets for several minutes. Remove to a wire rack to cool completely.

MAKES 3 DOZEN

QUICK PUMPKIN BARS

1	cup vegetable oil
4	eggs
2	cups sugar
2	cups canned pumpkin
2	cups flour
2	teaspoons baking powder
1	teaspoon baking soda
2	teaspoons cinnamon
½	teaspoon salt
	Cream Cheese Frosting

1 Combine the oil, eggs and sugar in a large mixer bowl and beat until smooth. Beat in the pumpkin. Add the flour, baking powder, baking soda, cinnamon and salt and mix well.

2 Spoon into an ungreased 10x15-inch baking pan. Bake at 350 degrees for 20 to 25 minutes or until a wooden pick inserted in the center comes out clean. Cool completely on a wire rack.

3 Spread with Cream Cheese Frosting. Let stand until the frosting is set. Cut into bars. Store, covered, in the refrigerator.

MAKES 3 DOZEN

Cream Cheese Frosting

6	tablespoons margarine, softened
3	ounces cream cheese, softened
2	cups confectioners' sugar
1	teaspoon milk
1	teaspoon vanilla extract

1 Cream the margarine and cream cheese in a mixer bowl until light.

2 Add the confectioners' sugar, milk and vanilla and beat until fluffy.

MAKES 2½ CUPS

In the eighteenth and nineteenth centuries, it was common to use fabrics "en suite"—using the same fabric for upholstery and windows.

RASPBERRY BARS

1   cup butter

1   cup packed brown sugar

1½ cups flour

1½ cups rolled oats

½   teaspoon baking soda

¼   teaspoon salt

1   cup chopped nuts

1   (10-ounce) jar raspberry jam

1   Melt the butter in a saucepan; remove from the heat. Stir in the brown sugar until dissolved. Cool to room temperature. Combine with the flour, oats, baking soda and salt in a bowl and mix well. Mix in the nuts.

2   Reserve 1 cup of the oat mixture for the topping. Press the remaining mixture into a greased 9x13-inch baking pan. Spread with the raspberry jam and sprinkle the reserved oat mixture over the top. Bake at 350 degrees for 30 minutes. Cool on a wire rack. Cut into bars.

MAKES 4 DOZEN

ROCCA

2   cups flour

1   cup packed brown sugar

1   teaspoon baking powder

½   teaspoon baking soda

1   teaspoon vanilla extract

1   cup butter, softened

1   large chocolate bar, broken

     chopped nuts

1   Combine the flour, brown sugar, baking powder, baking soda, vanilla and butter in a mixer bowl and beat until well mixed. Spread in a greased 10x15-inch baking pan. Bake at 275 degrees for 35 to 40 minutes or until brown.

2   Sprinkle with the chocolate and return to the oven until the chocolate melts, then spread evenly over the baked layer. Sprinkle with nuts. Let stand until cool. Cut into bars.

MAKES 4 TO 5 DOZEN

SOUR CREAM NUT HORNS

1	**cup butter, softened**
2	**cups flour, sifted**
1	**egg yolk**
¾	**cup sour cream**
1	**cup finely chopped walnuts or pecans**
1	**cup sugar**
1¼	**teaspoons cinnamon**
¼	**cup melted butter**

1 Cut the softened butter into the flour with a pastry blender in a bowl until crumbly. Blend the egg yolk with the sour cream in a small bowl. Add to the crumb mixture and mix well to form a dough. Wrap with foil and chill for 1 hour or longer.

2 Mix the walnuts, sugar, cinnamon and melted butter in a bowl.

3 Divide the chilled dough into 4 portions. Roll each portion into an 8-inch circle ⅛ inch thick on a floured and sugared surface. Top with the walnut mixture, spreading almost to the edges. Cut each circle into 12 wedges. Roll from the wide end, enclosing the nut filling.

4 Place on a cookie sheet. Bake at 375 degrees for 20 to 25 minutes or just until golden brown. Cool on the cookie sheet for several minutes. Remove to a wire rack to cool completely. Store in an airtight container or in the the freezer.

MAKES 4 DOZEN

TEATIME TASSIES

½	**cup butter, softened**
3	**ounces cream cheese, softened**
1	**cup sifted flour**
1	**egg**
¾	**cup packed brown sugar**
1	**tablespoon melted butter**
	salt to taste
1	**teaspoon vanilla extract**
⅔	**cup chopped pecans**

Tassies can also be filled with apricot or poppy seed filling.

1 Beat the softened butter and cream cheese in a mixer bowl until light. Add the flour and mix well. Shape into 24 balls. Press into ungreased 1½-inch muffin cups.

2 Beat the egg and brown sugar in a mixer bowl until smooth. Add the melted butter, salt, vanilla and pecans and mix well. Spoon into the prepared muffin cups.

3 Place the muffin pans on a baking sheet. Bake at 325 degrees for 25 minutes. Cool in the muffin pans on a wire rack for several minutes. Loosen with a knife and remove to the wire rack to cool completely.

MAKES 2 DOZEN

BANANA CAKE

$2\frac{1}{2}$ cups sifted cake flour

$1\frac{2}{3}$ cups sugar

$1\frac{1}{4}$ teaspoons baking powder

$1\frac{1}{4}$ teaspoons baking soda

1 teaspoon salt

$1\frac{1}{4}$ cups sliced bananas

$\frac{2}{3}$ cup butter, softened

$\frac{2}{3}$ cup buttermilk

2 eggs

$\frac{2}{3}$ cup chopped nuts

1 banana

2 cups whipping cream

2 tablespoons confectioners' sugar

1 teaspoon vanilla extract

2 bananas

1 Butter the bottoms and sides of two 9-inch cake pans. Line the bottoms with waxed paper and butter the waxed paper.

2 Sift the cake flour, sugar, baking powder, baking soda and salt into a large mixer bowl. Add $1\frac{1}{4}$ cups bananas, butter and $\frac{1}{3}$ cup of the buttermilk. Beat for 2 minutes, scraping the bowl occasionally.

3 Add the remaining $\frac{1}{3}$ cup buttermilk and eggs. Beat for 2 minutes, scraping the bowl occasionally. Fold in the nuts. Spoon the batter into the prepared cake pans. Bake at 350 degrees for 30 to 35 minutes or until the layers test done. Cool in the pans for 10 minutes. Remove to a wire rack to cool completely.

4 Slice 1 banana. Beat the whipping cream in a mixer bowl until soft peaks form. Add the confectioners' sugar and vanilla and mix well.

5 Place 1 cake layer on a serving plate. Arrange the 1 sliced banana over the layer. Spread half the whipped cream over the banana; do not spread over the side. Top with the remaining cake layer. Spread with the remaining whipped cream. Chill for several hours if desired.

6 Slice the remaining 2 bananas diagonally just before serving and arrange around the outer edge of the top. Store any leftovers in the refrigerator.

SERVES 12

Did you know that even George Washington had slipcovers in his home? These versatile covers for upholstered furniture work best on classic frame styles, such as rolled-arm sofas and club chairs, wingbacks, or furniture frames without a lot of exposed wood. Leather cannot be slipcovered (the fabric will slide), and fabrics with a latex backing should not be used for slipcovers.

CHOCOLATE FUDGE CAKE

3   ounces unsweetened chocolate

2¼ cups sifted cake flour

2   teaspoons baking soda

½   teaspoon salt

½   cup butter, softened

2½ cups packed light brown sugar

3   eggs

1½ teaspoons vanilla extract

1   cup sour cream

1   cup boiling water
     Chocolate Fudge Frosting

1 Grease and flour two 9-inch cake pans. Place the chocolate in a small bowl over hot water and let stand until melted. Sift the cake flour, baking soda and salt together.

2 Beat the butter in a mixer bowl until smooth. Add the brown sugar and eggs. Beat at high speed for 5 minutes or until light and fluffy. Add the melted chocolate and vanilla. Beat until blended. Add the dry ingredients alternately with the sour cream, beating with a wooden spoon after each addition until smooth. Stir in the boiling water.

3 Spoon into the prepared cake pans. Bake at 350 degrees for 35 minutes or until the centers spring back when lightly touched. Cool in the pans for 10 minutes. Remove to a wire rack to cool completely.

4 Spread Chocolate Fudge Frosting between the layers and over the top and side of the cake.

SERVES 12

Chocolate Fudge Frosting

4   ounces unsweetened chocolate

½   cup butter

1   (1-pound) package confectioners' sugar

½   cup milk

2   teaspoons vanilla extract

1 Combine the chocolate and butter in a small heavy saucepan. Melt over low heat, stirring frequently to blend well. Combine the confectioners' sugar, milk and vanilla in a bowl and mix well. Stir in the chocolate mixture.

2 Set the bowl in a pan of ice water. Beat with a wooden spoon until thickened and of a spreading consistency.

FROSTS ONE 2-LAYER CAKE

CHOCOLATE ZUCCHINI CAKE

4   ounces unsweetened chocolate

2   cups unbleached flour

1/3 cup baking cocoa

2   teaspoons baking soda

2   teaspoons baking powder

1   teaspoon salt

1/2 cup vegetable oil

1/2 cup butter, softened

2   cups sugar

3   eggs, beaten

1   tablespoon vanilla extract

1/3 cup buttermilk or sour cream

3   cups coarsely grated zucchini

1/2 cup chopped nuts (optional)

Cream Cheese Frosting

1 Melt the chocolate in a saucepan over low heat. Sift the flour, baking cocoa, baking soda, baking powder and salt together.

2 Beat the oil and butter in a mixer bowl until light and fluffy. Add the sugar, eggs and vanilla. Beat until blended. Beat in the chocolate. Add the flour mixture alternately with the buttermilk, stirring well after each addition. Fold in the zucchini and nuts.

3 Spoon into 2 greased and floured 9-inch cake pans. Bake at 350 degrees on the middle oven rack for 40 minutes or until a wooden pick inserted in the centers comes out clean. Cool in the pans for 10 minutes. Remove to a wire rack to cool completely.

4 Spread Cream Cheese Frosting between the layers and over the top and side of the cake.

SERVES 12

Cream Cheese Frosting

8   ounces cream cheese, softened

1/2 cup butter, softened

2   teaspoons vanilla extract

1   (1-pound) package confectioners' sugar

1 Beat the cream cheese, butter and vanilla in a mixer bowl until light and fluffy.

2 Add the confectioners' sugar, beating until the frosting is of a spreading consistency.

FROSTS ONE 2-LAYER CAKE

JAPANESE FRUIT CAKE

3⅓ cups sifted cake flour

1½ teaspoons baking powder

2 cups sugar

1 cup butter, softened

4 eggs

⅔ cup milk

1 teaspoon vanilla extract

1 cup chopped pecans

¾ cup dark raisins

1 teaspoon allspice

1 teaspoon cinnamon

¾ teaspoon ground cloves

Coconut Frosting

1 cup shredded fresh or canned coconut

1 Butter and flour three 9-inch cake pans. Sift the cake flour and baking powder together twice. Cream the sugar and 1 cup butter in a mixer bowl until light and fluffy. Beat in the eggs 1 at a time. Add the cake flour mixture and milk alternately, mixing well after each addition. Beat in the vanilla.

2 Spoon ⅓ of the batter into 1 of the prepared cake pans. Add the pecans, raisins, allspice, cinnamon and cloves to the remaining batter and mix well. Spoon into the remaining 2 pans. Bake at 350 degrees for 25 to 30 minutes or until the layers test done. Cool in the pans for 10 minutes. Remove to a wire rack to cool completely.

3 Layer the plain cake layer between the 2 pecan and raisin layers on a cake plate, spreading Coconut Frosting between layers. Spread the remaining frosting over the top and side of the cake. Sprinkle with the coconut.

SERVES 12 TO 16

Coconut Frosting

2 cups shredded fresh or canned coconut

2 cups sugar

1 cup water

⅓ cup fresh lemon juice

1 teaspoon grated lemon peel

½ cup water

3 tablespoons cornstarch

1 Combine the coconut, sugar, 1 cup water, lemon juice and lemon peel in a heavy saucepan and mix well. Bring to a boil, stirring frequently. Stir in a mixture of ½ cup water and cornstarch.

2 Cook over medium-low heat until the mixture mounds when dropped from a spoon, stirring constantly. Let stand until cool.

FROSTS ONE 3-LAYER CAKE

HAZELNUT CAKE

10 tablespoons butter, softened

1 cup minus 2 tablespoons sugar

4 eggs

1¼ cups hazelnuts, ground

¾ cup plus 2 tablespoons flour

2 teaspoons baking powder

1¼ cups confectioners' sugar

¼ cup baking cocoa

2 tablespoons melted butter

1 Beat the softened butter in a mixer bowl until light. Add the sugar 1 tablespoon at a time, beating well after each addition. Beat in the eggs 1 at a time.

2 Mix the hazelnuts, flour and baking powder in a bowl. Stir into the creamed mixture. Spoon into a greased loaf pan. Bake at 350 degrees for 45 minutes. Cool in the pan for 10 minutes. Remove to a wire rack to cool completely.

3 Beat the remaining ingredients in a bowl. Mix in enough hot water to make of glaze consistency. Drizzle over the cake.

SERVES 8 TO 10

OATMEAL CAKE

1 cup quick-cooking oats

1½ cups flour

1 teaspoon baking soda

1 teaspoon cinnamon

½ teaspoon salt

¼ teaspoon nutmeg

1 cup plus 2 tablespoons butter

1 cup sugar

1⅔ cups packed brown sugar

2 eggs

1 teaspoon vanilla extract

¼ cup cream

⅔ cup chopped walnuts

1 (3-ounce) can shredded coconut

1 Pour 1¼ cups boiling water over the oats in a bowl and mix well. Set aside. Mix the flour, baking soda, cinnamon, salt and nutmeg together.

2 Beat ½ cup of the softened butter in a mixer bowl until light. Add the sugar, 1 cup of the brown sugar, eggs and vanilla. Beat until blended, scraping the bowl occasionally. Add the oats, beating until mixed. Stir in the flour mixture.

3 Spoon into a buttered 9x11-inch cake pan. Bake at 350 degrees for 40 minutes.

4 Mix the remaining butter, remaining brown sugar and cream in a bowl. Stir in the walnuts and coconut. Spread over the hot cake. Broil for 5 minutes or until golden brown.

SERVES 15

PINEAPPLE UPSIDE-DOWN CAKE

½   cup butter

1   cup packed brown sugar

1   cup pineapple slices

    maraschino cherries

1   cup sifted flour

1   teaspoon baking powder

⅛   teaspoon salt

3   egg yolks

1   cup sugar

5   tablespoons pineapple juice

3   egg whites

1   Melt the butter in a large cast-iron skillet. Sprinkle with the brown sugar. Arrange the pineapple slices in a single layer in the brown sugar. Place a cherry in the center of each pineapple slice.

2   Sift the flour, baking powder and salt together. Beat the egg yolks in a mixer bowl until pale yellow. Add the sugar gradually, beating constantly until blended. Add the flour mixture and pineapple juice, mixing well.

3   Beat the egg whites in a mixer bowl until soft peaks form. Fold into the batter. Spoon into the prepared skillet.

4   Bake at 375 degrees for 30 to 35 minutes. Let stand for 5 minutes. Invert onto a serving platter.

SERVES 8 TO 10

POTATO CAKE

2   cups sifted cake flour

½   cup baking cocoa

2   teaspoons baking powder

½   teaspoon baking soda

½   teaspoon each nutmeg, cloves and cinnamon

1   cup chopped pecans

2   cups sugar

1   cup butter, softened

4   eggs

1   cup mashed cooked potatoes

1   teaspoon vanilla extract

½   cup milk

1   Sift the cake flour, baking cocoa, baking powder, baking soda, nutmeg, cloves and cinnamon together twice. Stir in the pecans.

2   Cream the sugar and butter in a mixer bowl until light and fluffy, scraping the bowl occasionally. Beat in the eggs 1 at a time. Add the potatoes and mix well. Stir in the vanilla. Add the flour mixture alternately with the milk, mixing well after each addition.

3   Spoon the batter into 4 buttered and floured 9-inch cake pans. Bake at 350 degrees for 25 to 30 minutes or until the layers test done. Cool in the pans for 10 minutes. Remove to a wire rack to cool completely. Frost with 7-minute frosting and decorate with pecan halves.

SERVES 12

PEAR CAKE

2   cups flour

2   teaspoons baking soda

½   teaspoon cinnamon

1   cup packed brown sugar

¾   cup plain yogurt

½   cup orange juice

¼   cup butter, softened

3   eggs

2   teaspoons grated orange peel

3   pears, peeled, grated

      Caramel Frosting

1   Sift the flour, baking soda and cinnamon together. Beat the brown sugar, yogurt, orange juice, butter, eggs and orange peel in a mixer bowl until smooth. Add the flour mixture and mix well. Stir in the pears.

2   Spoon into a greased 9x13-inch cake pan. Bake at 350 degrees for 45 minutes. Cool in the pan on a wire rack. Spread with the Caramel Frosting.

SERVES 15

Caramel Frosting

¼   cup butter

½   cup packed brown sugar

2   tablespoons cream

¾   cup plus 3 tablespoons confectioners' sugar

1   Melt the butter in a saucepan. Add the brown sugar and mix well. Cook over low heat for 2 minutes, stirring constantly. Stir in the cream.

2   Bring to a boil and remove from the heat. Add the confectioners' sugar, beating until blended. Cool slightly.

FROSTS ONE 9X13-INCH CAKE

BROWN SUGAR POUND CAKE

3	cups flour
1	teaspoon baking powder
½	teaspoon salt
1	(1-pound) package brown sugar
1	cup sugar
1	cup margarine, softened
½	cup shortening
5	eggs
1	cup milk
1	teaspoon vanilla extract
1	cup chopped walnuts

1 Sift the flour, baking powder and salt together. Cream the brown sugar, sugar, margarine and shortening in a mixer bowl until light and fluffy, scraping the bowl occasionally. Beat in the eggs. Add the flour mixture alternately with the milk and vanilla, mixing well after each addition. Stir in the walnuts.

2 Spoon into a greased and floured tube pan. Bake at 350 degrees for 1¼ hours or until the cake tests done. Cool in the pan for several minutes. Invert onto a wire rack to cool completely.

SERVES 16

LEMON POUND CAKE

1½	cups flour
2	teaspoons grated lemon peel
¼	teaspoon baking powder
⅛	teaspoon baking soda
⅓	cup butter, softened
1	cup sugar
4	egg whites
2	tablespoons lemon juice
½	teaspoon each lemon and vanilla extract
⅔	cup low-fat plain yogurt
	juice of 1 lemon
1½	tablespoons sugar

1 Mix the flour, lemon peel, baking powder and baking soda together. Beat the butter in a mixer bowl. Add 1 cup sugar gradually, beating constantly for 10 minutes or until light and fluffy.

2 Add the egg whites, 2 tablespoons lemon juice and flavorings, beating until blended. Add the flour mixture alternately with the yogurt, beating just until blended; do not overbeat.

3 Spoon into a greased and floured 4x8-inch or 5x9-inch loaf pan. Bake at 325 degrees for 1 to 1¼ hours or until the cake tests done. Cool in the pan for 10 minutes. Remove to a wire rack to cool completely. Brush with a mixture of the juice of 1 lemon and 1½ tablespoons sugar.

4 Do not substitute for the butter in this recipe.

SERVES 8 TO 10

RUM CAKE

1   (2-layer) package yellow butter cake mix

1   package vanilla instant pudding mix

½   cup vegetable oil

½   cup light rum

½   cup water

4   eggs

½   cup chopped pecans (optional)

½   cup butter

1   cup sugar

¼   cup rum

¼   cup water

1   Combine the cake mix, pudding mix, oil, ½ cup light rum and ½ cup water in a bowl and mix until smooth. Add the eggs 1 at a time and beat for 2 to 3 minutes. Stir in the pecans.

2   Spoon into a greased and floured bundt pan. Bake at 325 degrees for 45 to 60 minutes or until a tester inserted in the cake comes out clean. Cool in the pan on a wire rack. Loosen the cake with a soft spatula and invert onto a cake plate.

3   Melt the butter in a saucepan. Stir in the sugar, ¼ cup rum and ¼ cup water. Bring to a boil, stirring to blend well. Pierce the cake with a wooden pick and pour the glaze slowly over the cake.

SERVES 16

Sofas have moved beyond the living room and family room. With all the styles and scales of upholstered furniture available today, consider placing a sofa in the master bedroom, the kitchen (so guests can relax while they talk to the cook), or even a settee or loveseat in a luxurious bathroom.

SACHERTORTE

8   **ounces finely ground walnuts**

⅓   **cup flour**

1   **cup unsalted butter, softened**

1   **cup sugar**

2   **teaspoons vanilla extract**

¾   **teaspoon salt**

8   **egg yolks**

8   **(1-ounce) squares semisweet chocolate, melted, cooled to lukewarm**

8   **egg whites**

⅔   **cup apricot jam**

     Mocha Frosting

     sweetened whipped cream

1   Toss the walnuts with the flour in a bowl. Cream the butter, sugar, vanilla and salt in a mixer bowl until light and fluffy. Beat in the egg yolks 1 at a time. Stir in the chocolate and walnuts.

2   Beat the egg whites in a mixer bowl until soft peaks form. Stir ¼ of the egg whites into the chocolate mixture. Fold in the remaining egg whites.

3   Spoon into a buttered and floured 9-inch springform pan. Bake at 350 degrees for 1 hour. Cool in the pan on a wire rack for 20 minutes. Push down the side of the cake so it is flush with the middle. Let stand until completely cool. Invert onto a serving platter lined with half sheets of waxed paper that can be removed after frosting the cake.

4   Heat the apricot jam in a saucepan. Press through a sieve. Brush the side and top of the cake with the jam. Let stand for 30 minutes or until the glaze sets.

5   Pour the Mocha Frosting over the cake, rotating the cake while spreading the frosting evenly with a spatula. Chill until set. Remove the waxed paper. Bring the cake to room temperature before serving. Serve with sweetened whipped cream. Garnish as desired. For variety, add 1½ cups coarsely chopped fresh cranberries and 1 tablespoon grated orange peel to the batter with the chocolate.

SERVES 12

Mocha Frosting

½   **cup whipping cream**

2   **teaspoons instant coffee granules**

6   **(1-ounce) squares semisweet chocolate, chopped**

1   Scald the whipping cream in a saucepan. Whisk in the coffee granules and chocolate. Cook for 1 minute, whisking constantly.

2   Remove from the heat and stir until the chocolate melts. Let stand until just warm.

FROSTS 1 SACHERTORTE

SHERRY CAKE

1 (2-layer) package yellow cake mix

1 (4-ounce) package vanilla instant
pudding mix

¾ cup vegetable oil

¾ cup cream sherry

4 eggs

½ cup chopped pecans (optional)
Sherry Glaze
confectioners' sugar to taste

1 Combine the cake mix, pudding mix, oil and cream sherry in a mixer bowl. Beat at low speed just until moistened, scraping the bowl occasionally. Beat in the eggs 1 at a time. Beat at high speed for 5 minutes, scraping the bowl occasionally. Fold in the pecans.

2 Spoon into a greased and floured 10-cup bundt pan. Bake at 325 degrees for 55 minutes. Cool in the pan on a wire rack for 10 minutes.

3 Pierce the cake with a wooden skewer and drizzle with half the Sherry Glaze. Let stand for several minutes. Invert the cake onto a serving platter. Drizzle with the remaining Sherry Glaze. Sift confectioners' sugar over the cooled cake.

SERVES 16

Sherry Glaze

1 cup confectioners' sugar

¼ cup cream sherry

1 Combine the confectioners' sugar and cream sherry in a bowl.

2 Mix until smooth.

MAKES 1 CUP

If you live in a cold climate or want extra-luxurious window treatments, consider *interlining*, a flannel-like fabric that is sandwiched between the decorative face fabric and the lining. Interlining traps air, prevents drafts, and, not incidentally, makes a drapery look like a million bucks. Interlining also works to prevent heat buildup in warmer climates.

WALNUT PUMPKIN ROLL

1   **cup cake flour**

2   **teaspoons cinnamon**

1   **teaspoon baking soda**

3   **eggs**

1   **cup sugar**

2/3   **cup canned pumpkin**

1   **cup walnut pieces**

8   **ounces cream cheese, softened**

1/4   **cup butter or margarine, softened**

1½   **cups confectioners' sugar**

¾   **teaspoon vanilla extract**

A wonderful alternative to pumpkin pie.

1   Line a 10x15-inch baking pan with foil and grease the foil. Mix the cake flour, cinnamon and baking soda together.

2   Beat the eggs in a mixer bowl at high speed for 5 minutes or until thickened and pale yellow. Add the sugar and pumpkin gradually, beating constantly until blended. Add the cake flour mixture gradually, beating just until smooth.

3   Spread evenly in the prepared pan. Sprinkle with the walnuts. Bake at 375 degrees for 10 to 15 minutes or until a wooden pick inserted in the center comes out clean.

4   Loosen the cake from the edges of the pan immediately. Invert onto a dish towel sprinkled generously with confectioners' sugar; discard the foil. Roll the hot cake and towel from the narrow end. Cool on a wire rack.

5   Beat the cream cheese and butter in a mixer bowl at medium speed until light. Add 1½ cups confectioners' sugar and vanilla and mix until smooth. Unroll the cake and spread with the cream cheese mixture. Reroll and wrap in plastic wrap. Chill for 2 hours. Sprinkle with additional confectioners' sugar and cut into 10 to 12 slices.

SERVES 10 TO 12

SWEDISH APPLE PIE

3 pounds (or more) Cortland or
   Delicious apples, peeled, cut into
   ¼-inch slices
1 tablespoon sugar
1 tablespoon cinnamon
1 unbaked (10-inch) deep-dish
   pie shell
1 cup flour
1 cup sugar
⅛ teaspoon salt
¾ cup melted butter
1 egg, beaten
½ cup chopped walnuts or pecans

1 Toss the apples with a mixture of 1 tablespoon sugar and the cinnamon in a bowl. Spoon into the pie shell, mounding the apples 1 inch higher in the center than at the edge of the pie plate.

2 Mix the flour, 1 cup sugar and salt in a bowl. Stir in the butter and egg. Fold in the walnuts.

3 Spread over the apple mixture and press lightly. Bake at 350 degrees for 45 to 50 minutes or until the apples are tender.

SERVES 6 TO 8

Don't go crazy trying to match colors within a fabric. Designer Mario Buatta taught us that the best coordinating color is usually an in-between color— not an actual color in a pattern, but one that is a blend of the colors that you see when you step back and squint your eyes. This will give you a more sophisticated color palette for the room.

CHOCOLATE ANGEL PIE

2	egg whites
1/8	teaspoon salt
1/8	teaspoon cream of tartar
1/2	cup sugar
1/2	cup finely chopped pecans
1/2	teaspoon vanilla extract
4	ounces German's chocolate, chopped
3	tablespoons water
1	cup whipping cream
1	teaspoon vanilla extract

1 Beat the egg whites, salt and cream of tartar in a mixer bowl until foamy. Add the sugar 2 tablespoons at a time, beating constantly until stiff peaks form. Fold in the pecans and 1/2 teaspoon vanilla.

2 Spoon into a lightly buttered 8-inch pie plate, building up the side 1/2 inch above the edge of the pie plate to form a shell. Bake at 300 degrees for 50 to 55 minutes or until light brown. Cool on a wire rack.

3 Combine the chocolate and water in a saucepan. Cook over low heat until blended, stirring frequently. Let stand until cool.

4 Beat the whipping cream in a mixer bowl until soft peaks form. Add 1 teaspoon vanilla and mix well. Fold into the chocolate mixture. Spoon into the prepared pie shell. Chill for 2 hours.

SERVES 6 TO 8

CHOCOLATE CHEESE PIE

9	ounces chocolate chip cookies, finely crushed
1/2	cup melted margarine
24	ounces cream cheese, softened
3/4	cup sugar
4	eggs
1	cup milk chocolate chips, melted, cooled
1	cup sour cream
1/2	cup amaretto
1/4	cup margarine, softened
1	teaspoon vanilla extract
1	cup whipping cream, whipped

1 Mix the cookie crumbs and 1/2 cup margarine in a bowl. Press the crumb mixture over the bottom and up the side of a pie plate. Chill in the refrigerator.

2 Beat the cream cheese and sugar in a mixer bowl until light and fluffy, scraping the bowl occasionally. Beat in the eggs 1 at a time. Stir in the chocolate, sour cream, amaretto, 1/4 cup margarine and vanilla.

3 Spoon into the prepared pie plate. Bake at 350 degrees for 65 minutes or until set. Cool on a wire rack. Serve with the whipped cream.

SERVES 6 TO 8

LEMON CRUNCH PIE

1 cup sugar

3 tablespoons cornstarch

⅛ teaspoon salt

grated peel and juice of 1 lemon

2 egg yolks, beaten

¼ cup water

1 cup boiling water

2 egg whites

1 baked (9-inch) pie shell

¾ cup flour

2 tablespoons sugar

¼ teaspoon baking powder

¼ cup margarine, softened

1 Combine 1 cup sugar, cornstarch and salt in a microwave-safe bowl. Stir in the lemon peel and lemon juice. Whisk the egg yolks and ¼ cup water in a small bowl. Stir into the lemon mixture. Add 1 cup boiling water and mix well with a wooden spoon.

2 Microwave on High for 2 minutes; stir. Microwave on Medium for 1 minute; stir. Microwave on Medium for up to 5 minutes or until thickened and clear, stirring at 1-minute intervals.

3 Beat the egg whites in a mixer bowl until stiff peaks form. Fold the hot lemon mixture very gradually into the egg whites. Spoon into the pie shell.

4 Mix the flour, 2 tablespoons sugar and baking powder in a bowl. Cut in the margarine until crumbly. Sprinkle the crumb mixture over the top of the prepared layer. Bake at 400 degrees for 15 minutes or until golden brown.

SERVES 6 TO 8

When designing window treatments, think in terms of the room, not just the window. Sometimes it helps to remove existing window dressings—draperies, curtains, shades, blinds, rods, hardware—in order to visualize all the possibilities.

GREEN TOMATO PIE

2	all ready pie pastries
½	cup sugar
½	cup packed brown sugar
5	tablespoons flour
2	tablespoons lemon juice
½	teaspoon cinnamon
½	teaspoon nutmeg
¼	teaspoon salt
4	cups thinly sliced peeled green tomatoes

1 Line a 9-inch pie plate with 1 of the pastries. Mix the sugar, brown sugar, flour, lemon juice, cinnamon, nutmeg and salt in a bowl. Add the tomatoes, tossing to coat.

2 Spoon the tomato mixture into the prepared pie plate. Top with the remaining pastry, sealing the edge and cutting vents.

3 Bake at 400 degrees for 50 to 60 minutes or until golden brown. Cool slightly on a wire rack. Serve warm.

SERVES 6 TO 8

MINCEMEAT PIES

5	unpeeled medium-large apples, cut into quarters, seeded
1	cup seedless raisins
½	unpeeled lemon, seeded
1	cup currants
2	teaspoons cinnamon
¾	teaspoon ground cloves
¾	teaspoon nutmeg
½	teaspoon salt
2	tablespoons unbleached flour
⅔	to 1 cup sugar or equivalent sugar substitute
⅓	cup brandy
4	all ready pie pastries

Decrease the spices by ⅓ to ½ for a less spicy mincemeat, or substitute 1½ teaspoons rum for the brandy. The mincemeat mixture can also be used in cookies.

1 Combine the apples, raisins and lemon in a food processor fitted with a steel blade. Process until coarsely ground. Add the currants, cinnamon, cloves, nutmeg, salt, flour and sugar. Process until mixed. Stir in the brandy. Let stand at room temperature for 1 hour.

2 Line two 8-inch pie plates with 2 of the pastries. Spoon the mincemeat mixture into the pie plates. Top with the remaining pastries, sealing the edges and cutting vents.

3 Bake at 475 degrees for 15 minutes. Reduce the oven temperature to 375 degrees. Bake for 50 minutes longer or until the centers of the pastries are brown. Let stand until cool.

MAKES 2 PIES

PURPLE PLUM PIE

1   cup sugar

¼   cup flour

1   to 2 tablespoons cinnamon

1   unbaked (9-inch) pie shell

20   to 21 purple prune plums, cut into halves, pits removed

2   tablespoons butter or margarine

Purple prune plums, sometimes called Italian plums, are brilliant in color and available for only a few weeks in August and September.

1   Mix the sugar, flour and cinnamon in a bowl. Sprinkle ¼ of the mixture over the bottom of the pie shell. Arrange the plum halves in concentric circles in the prepared pie shell. Sprinkle with the remaining sugar mixture. Dot with the butter.

2   Bake at 425 degrees for 10 minutes. Reduce the oven temperature to 350 degrees. Bake for 30 to 35 minutes longer.

SERVES 6 TO 8

A color and fabric for a window treatment that will harmonize with the room should either be the same color as the walls (or darker or lighter versions thereof), the same color as the major upholstery, or the accent color of the room that is used on small chairs, pillows, and accessories.

WORLD CLASS PUMPKIN PIE

3   eggs

⅔   cup sugar

⅔   cup packed brown sugar

2   cups canned pumpkin

1½ teaspoons cinnamon

1   teaspoon ginger

½   teaspoon ground cloves

½   teaspoon allspice

¼   teaspoon cardamom

⅛   teaspoon salt

¾   cup whipping cream

¾   cup half-and-half

1½ tablespoons bourbon or dark rum
     (optional)
     Pie Pastry

3   tablespoons butter, softened

⅔   cup chopped pecans

. . . or the very best pumpkin pie ever eaten!

1   Beat the eggs, sugar and ⅓ cup of the brown sugar in a mixer bowl until light and fluffy. Stir in the pumpkin, cinnamon, ginger, cloves, allspice, cardamom and salt. Add the whipping cream, half-and-half and bourbon and mix well.

2   Spoon into a pie plate lined with Pie Pastry. Bake at 450 degrees for 8 minutes. Reduce the oven temperature to 325 degrees. Bake for 40 to 45 minutes or until set.

3   Mix the remaining ⅓ cup brown sugar, butter and pecans in a bowl. Sprinkle over the pie. Broil just until brown.

SERVES 6 TO 8

Pie Pastry

1¼ cups unbleached flour

1   teaspoon sugar

½   teaspoon salt

¼   cup unsalted butter, chilled

3   tablespoons vegetable shortening,
     chilled

2½ to 3 tablespoons ice water

1   Sift the flour, sugar and salt into a bowl. Cut in the butter and shortening until crumbly. Add the ice water 1 tablespoon at a time, mixing with a fork until the mixture forms a ball. Chill, wrapped in waxed paper, for 2 hours.

2   Roll the dough into a 12-inch circle on a lightly floured surface. Fit into a 9-inch pie plate; crimp the edge.

MAKES 1 PIE SHELL

Pear Tart

1	cup unbleached flour
½	cup unsalted butter, chilled, chopped
1½	tablespoons sugar
⅛	teaspoon salt
2	to 3 tablespoons ice water
5	or 6 peeled medium-ripe pear halves
5	tablespoons sugar
¼	cup unsalted butter
1	tablespoon Poire Williams or other pear liqueur
⅓	cup apricot jam
2	tablespoons Poire Williams or other pear liqueur
	whipped cream
	Poire Williams or other pear liqueur to taste

1 Combine the flour, ½ cup butter, 1½ tablespoons sugar and salt in a food processor fitted with a steel blade. Process until crumbly. Add the ice water gradually, processing constantly until the mixture forms a ball. Chill, wrapped with plastic wrap, for 1 hour or longer.

2 Roll the dough into a 12-inch circle on a lightly floured surface. Fit into a 9-inch tart pan; trim and crimp the edge. Prick the bottom with a fork. Place in the freezer.

3 Cut each of the pear halves crosswise into very thin slices, maintaining the shape of the pear half by keeping the slices in place. Fan 4 of the pear halves into a large blossom design in the prepared tart pan, filling in the holes with the fifth pear half. Sprinkle with 5 tablespoons sugar. Dot with the butter. Sprinkle with 1 tablespoon liqueur.

4 Bake at 400 degrees for 50 to 60 minutes or until the pears are caramelized and the crust is light brown. Cool for 10 minutes.

5 Heat the apricot jam and 2 tablespoons liqueur in a saucepan until blended, stirring frequently. Brush glaze over the top of the tart. Cut into wedges. Serve warm with whipped cream flavored with liqueur to taste.

SERVES 6 TO 8

Dry cleaning is highly recommended to clean slipcovers. A slipcover made with multiple components—fabric, welting, zippers, and lining—may shrink in varying degrees if washed.

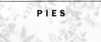

CHOCOLATE STRAWBERRY TART

1²/₃ cups unbleached flour

¼ cup superfine sugar

½ teaspoon salt

¾ cup unsalted butter, chilled

2 egg yolks, beaten

2 teaspoons cold water

1 teaspoon vanilla extract

1 cup semisweet chocolate chips or chopped dark chocolate

3 tablespoons kirsch

2 tablespoons melted unsalted butter

¼ cup confectioners' sugar, sifted

1 tablespoon water

2½ pints fresh whole strawberries

½ cup strawberry jelly, heated
  sprigs of fresh mint

1 Sift the flour, sugar and salt into a bowl. Cut in ¾ cup butter until crumbly. Stir in a mixture of the egg yolks, 2 teaspoons cold water and vanilla. Shape into a ball. Knead lightly on a lightly floured surface. Shape into a ball. Chill, wrapped with waxed paper, for 2 to 3 hours.

2 Roll the dough into a 12- to 14-inch circle on a lightly floured surface. Fit into a 10-inch tart pan with removable bottom, leaving a ¾-inch overhang. Fold the edge over to the inside and press into place. Chill in the refrigerator.

3 Line the bottom of the prepared tart pan with foil or waxed paper; weight with beans. Cover the edge with foil. Bake at 425 degrees for 8 minutes. Remove the foil and beans. Prick the bottom with a fork several times. Bake for 8 to 10 minutes longer or until the edge is light brown. Let stand until cool.

4 Melt the chocolate in a double boiler over simmering water, stirring frequently. Add kirsch and 2 tablespoons butter, stirring until blended. Add the confectioners' sugar and 1 tablespoon water and mix well. Spoon into the tart shell.

5 Arrange the strawberries with the tips up in a circular pattern over the warm chocolate filling. Brush with the warm jelly. Chill, covered, for 2 hours. Let stand at room temperature for 45 minutes before serving. Top with mint.

SERVES 8

PECAN CARAMEL TART

2 cups walnuts

½ cup blanched almonds

3 tablespoons sugar

6 tablespoons butter

1 teaspoon vanilla extract

1¾ cups pecan halves

¾ cup water

¾ cup sugar

7 tablespoons whipping cream

2 tablespoons bittersweet chocolate, melted

2 tablespoons whipping cream

1 Process the walnuts in a food processor until finely ground. Process the almonds and 3 tablespoons sugar in a food processor until of a powdery consistency.

2 Beat the butter in a mixer bowl until light and fluffy. Add the walnuts, almond mixture and vanilla and mix well. Press over the bottom and side of a 9-inch tart pan. Bake at 350 degrees for 20 to 25 minutes. Let stand until cool.

3 Toast the pecan halves on a baking sheet at 350 degrees for 8 to 10 minutes or until golden brown. Combine the water and ¾ cup sugar in a 2-quart saucepan. Cook for 12 to 15 minutes, washing sugar crystals from side of pan with a wet brush; do not stir. Bring to a boil. Boil for 5 to 7 minutes or until golden brown. Remove from the heat.

4 Stir in 7 tablespoons whipping cream 1 tablespoon at a time. Add the pecan halves and mix well. Spoon into the prepared tart pan. Drizzle with a mixture of the chocolate and 2 tablespoons whipping cream. Let stand at room temperature until set.

SERVES 8

Keep design files by room or by subject—for example, window treatments. As you read magazines, tear out pages and place them in your files. When it's time to decorate, you'll have lots of inspiration—and all of it to your taste.

CONTRIBUTOR LIST

Deborah Abrego-Valdez, Houston (Champions), TX
Jo Adamczyk, Bloomfield Hills, MI
Joyce Allen, Southwest District Manager
Barbara Anderson, Wilmington, DE
Karen Anderson, Salt Lake City, UT
Margaret Andrews, Avon, CT
Faith Andrianopoulos, Wilmington, DE
Charlotte Armstrong, Richmond, VA
Sally Anne Artese, Pasadena, CA
Janine Attia, Buffalo, NY
Elaine Axelband, Boca Raton, FL
Judy Baker, Wilmington, DE
Meredith Banta, Chicago, IL
Jane Barnhart, Marietta, GA
Catharine Barry, Denver, CO
Denise Battaglia, Buffalo, NY
Stacey Becker, Marietta, GA
Karen Becnel, Kennett Square, PA
Pat Bennett, Bellevue, WA
Ava Lee Bernish, Ramsey, NJ
Mary Beth Berry, Strafford, PA
Sharon Berry, Indianapolis, IN
Barbara Bible, Ft. Worth, TX
Kathy Biddle, Jenkintown, PA
Karla Bishop, Jenkintown, PA
Cristy Bisker, Rockville, MD
Jan Bobal, Marietta, GA
Cheryl Bolden, Birmingham, AL
Courtney Bolen, Okemos, MI
William Bolger, Osprey, FL
Caroline Bolin, Rochester, NY
Cheryl Bouvier, Los Altos, CA
Kathy Brady, Deerfield, IL
Susan Brady, Kennett Square, PA
Vickie Brand, Denver, CO
Karen Brink, Charlotte, NC
Kathleen Bruce, Bloomfield Hills, MI
Alta Bryant, Bloomfield Hills, MI
Martine Buhmann, Dallas, TX
Patricia Burnside, Santa Rosa, CA
Rena Byers, Charlotte, NC
Pam Cairns, Alexandria, VA

Ronnie Carolan, St. Louis, MO
Karen Chase, Sugar Land, TX
Roxie Cherry, Sugar Land, TX
Janet Codichini, Kennett Square, PA
India Cofer, Charlotte, NC
Fran Coleman, Shaker Heights, OH
Jeanne Collins, Westport, CT
Joyce Colman, Alexandria, VA
Gail Comiskey, Kansas City, KS
Sharon Connor, San Antonio, TX
Bonnie Cornwell, Alexandria, VA
Roxanne Corridan, Pleasant Hill, CA
Cathy Cotter, Wilmette, IL
Jean Coulbourne, Kennett Square, PA
Jackie Craig, Rochester, NY
Cheryl Crowley, Salt Lake City, UT
Elisabeth Cruickshank, Northwest District Manager
Mary Culbertson, Englewood, CO
Esmé Culotta, Sugar Land, TX
J. D. Daley, Englewood, CO
Mary D'Amelio, East Hanover, NJ
Judy Darr, Charlotte, NC
Carole Davidson, Salt Lake City, UT
Terri Day, Richmond, VA
Betty Deeley, Osprey, FL
Sherry Deems, Richmond, VA
Pat Delp, Indianapolis, IN
Colleen Delpo, Timonium, MD
Virginia Dole, Arcadia, CA
Janice Downey, Alexandria, VA
Angela Dreyer, Lynnwood, WA
Colleen Durham, Richmond, VA
Susan Eagan, San Antonio, TX
Bobi Jo Earnest, Englewood, CO
Ann Edwards, Edina, MN
Mary Elrick, Greenbrae, CA
Sue Evans, Annapolis, MD
Kris Faries, Kennett Square, PA
Susan Farrell-Melick, Albany, NY
Kay Faulman, Osprey, FL
Kirsten Feldstein, Jenkintown, PA

Tina Ferencz, Pleasant Hill, CA
Delia Ferrato, San Antonio, TX
Elsbeth Feys, Rockville, MD
Helen Floyd, Houston, TX
Nancy Foreacre, Kennett Square, PA
Nancy Forlino, Kennett Square, PA
Pat Forsha, Central District Manager
Bonnie Franzoni, Bloomfield Hills, MI
Sherri Frederick, Laguna Hills, CA
Mary Jane Friday, Reading, PA
Joy Funston, Stuart, FL
Lynn Gallop, Avon, CT
Suzanne Gawronski, Buffalo, NY
Joanne Gehman, River Edge, NJ
Francesca Giacalone, Santa Rosa, CA
Ski Gieshewski, Studio City, CA
Doris Gilgus, Kansas City, KS
Rebecca Reece Gilley, Kennett Square, PA
Julia Gily, Birmingham, AL
Tonnie Glover, Birmingham, AL
Graham Gold, Buckhead, GA
Joanne Gold, Buckhead, GA
Barbara Goldhammer, Bellevue, WA
Nazarita Goldhammer, Portland, OR
Dawn Gorman, Hinsdale, IL
Barbara Greenwood, Tulsa, OK
Pat Hackney, Stuart, FL
Becky Hall, Rockville, MD
Marilyn Hamann, Charlotte, NC
Karen Hanna, San Antonio, TX
Terri Hansen, Jacksonville, FL
Bekki Hargreaves, Denver, CO
Claudia Harman, Salt Lake City, UT
Trish Harper, Birmingham, AL
Uta Harrington, Greenbrae, CA
Arlene Harris, Shaker Heights, OH
Ken Harris, Houston, TX
Debbie Hart, Pasadena, CA
Linda Hawkins, Timonium, MD

Virginia Hayden, Houston, TX
Charlene Headley, Peabody, MA
Lorraine Healy, Greenbrae, CA
Terry Hebert, Albany, NY
Shirley Heermann, St. Louis, MO
Myra Heffron, Carle Place, NY
Heather Heizman, Kansas City, KS
Shawn Hermansen, Bloomfield Hills, MI
Mary Hernandez, Ft. Worth, TX
Diana Hibbs, Yardley, PA
Susan Hines, Kansas City, KS
Erika Hirling, Charlotte, NC
Karen Hirling, Charlotte, NC
Celia Hirsch, Boca Raton, FL
Carole Holland, Princeton, NJ
Ruth Holt, Wilmington, DE
Nancy Horton, Okemos, MI
Candace Howard, Peabody, MA
Helen Howick, Bellevue, WA
Judi Hughes, Santa Rosa, CA
Nancy Hummel, Reading, PA
Nancy Immenschuh, Kansas City, KS
Nell Jacks, Birmingham, AL
Diane James, Plano, TX
Barbra Jarzabek, Shaker Heights, OH
Linda Jean, Pleasant Hill, CA
Margaret Jendrejzak, Buffalo, NY
Jan Jessup, Kennett Square, PA
Susan Jimenez, Pasadena, CA
Jan Johnson, Englewood, CO
Carrie Jones, Jacksonville, FL
Ellison Jones, Pleasant Hill, CA
Kim Jones, Kennett Square, PA
Kathleen Jordan-Hart, Carle Place, NY
Kathy Joy, Okemos, MI
Anne Jung, Kennett Square, PA
Cheryl Junker, Las Vegas, NV
Sally Kaspar, Huntington Beach, CA
Peg Kriebel, Fairfax, VA
Theresa Labanara, Huntington Station, NY
Ruth Laughner, Rockville, MD
Emily Lavelle, Birmingham, AL
Tom Lawler, Studio City, CA

Carol Lear, Redwood City, CA
Mary Elise Leddy, Carle Place, NY
Roberta Levine, Carle Place, NY
Ginny Lewis, Louisiana/Texas District Manager
Darlene Lindell, Kennett Square, PA
Joan Lissner, San Diego, CA
Bonni Lopez, Novi, MI
Sue Lowden, Jacksonville, FL
Barbara Lunger, Frazer, PA
Noni Macon, New York/New England District Manager
Carole Lee Mafi, Pasadena, CA
Sally Maguire, Dallas, TX
Angelina Maher, Houston, TX
Connie Malette, Southeast District Manager
Pat Maloney, Huntington Beach, CA
Liz Marcolini, Albany, NY
Charlotte Massey, Houston, TX
Anne Mathes, New Orleans, LA
Duke Mattern, Ramsey, NJ
Pam Ruby Matulich, Las Vegas, NV
Laura McCracken, Kennett Square, PA
Michelle McDaniel, Jacksonville, FL
Kimberly McKeown, Kennett Square, PA
Cindy McLaurin, Falls Church, VA
Vickie Meranda, Alexandria, VA
Kathy Mikros, Bloomfield Hills, MI
Edie Miles, Marietta, GA
Nanette Miller, Buffalo, NY
Linda Modrall, Indianapolis, IN
Eldonna Moran, Sacramento, CA
Betty Morrison, Birmingham, AL
Margie Mueller, Denver, CO
Paula Murphy, Torrance, CA

Marion Nappi, Kennett Square, PA
Sopiko Nasidze, Saratoga, CA
Nicky Naushahi, Albany, NY
Mary Beth Newcomb, Plano, TX
Pat Nickels, Bloomfield Hills, MI
Coleen Norris, Alexandria, VA
Mimi Olson, Newark, DE
Susan Solinsky-Ort, Greenbrae, CA
Linda Panaggio, Stuart, FL
Sonia Parmet, Carle Place, NY
Elizabeth Passman, Wilmette, IL
Jill Pernsteiner, Charlotte, NC
Joyce Pettit, Marietta, GA
Kay Petz, Strafford, PA
Janet Phillips, Kennett Square, PA
Barb Piazza, Shaker Heights, OH
Barbara Ponzo, Deerfield, IL
Connie Purcell, Annapolis, MD
Judie Queen, Philadelphia District Manager
Tammie Rachou, Rockville, MD
Jan Ragan, Okemos, MI
Maxine Ranicke, Bellevue, WA
Faye Rasmussen, Jacksonville, FL
John Rica, Stuart, FL
Grace Ridgeway, Arlington, VA
Elaine Riggs, Bellevue, WA
Jason Riggs, Wilmington, DE
Nancy Rishforth, Boca Raton, FL
Zora Roades, Denver, CO
Vicki Roberts, Birmingham, AL
Eileen Robertson, Novi, MI
Vicki Robertson, Denver, CO
Diane Robinson, Houston, TX
Lenore Ruckman, Greenbrae, CA
Tina Ruggiero, Wilmington, DE
Rita Ryan, Huntington Station, NY
Aileen and Carolyn Salamone, New Orleans, LA
Trudy Sanclaria, Denver, CO
Maria Schandor, Houston, TX
Quita Schillhammer, Acton, MA

Toni Schirmer, Reading, PA
Susan Schlobohm, Brookfield, WI
Steve Schneider, Austin, TX
Linda Schoepf, Salt Lake City, UT
Liane Schraudner, Indianapolis, IN
Nancy Schuring, Saratoga, CA
Jan Scott, Torrance, CA
Vanessa Sepeter, Okemos, MI
Ed Sheppard, Washington, DC
Pat Sheridan, Annapolis, MD
Pat Shirley, Austin, TX
William Shuiler, Jr., Buffalo, NY
Eileen Silk, Cherry Hill, NJ
Marina Silva, Stuart, FL
Gail Sinnett, Charlotte, NC
Sharon Slater, Charlotte, NC
Coni Smith, Bloomfield Hills, MI
Jeanne Smith, Houston (Champions), TX
Peggy Smith, Charlotte, NC
Denise Snakard, Wilmette, IL
Joan Snow, Boca Raton, FL
Donna Sparano, Yardley, PA
Joan Stavert, Sugar Land, TX
Sharon Steeg, Ramsey, NJ
Becky Steele, Kennett Square, PA
Bill Steig, Strafford, PA
Kathy Steppling, Charlotte, NC
Virginia Stone, Sacramento, CA
Jane Strange, Fairfax, VA
Holly Stroud, Charlotte, NC
Polly Stroud, Charlotte, NC
Sue Summers, Kansas City, KS
Tina Swindler, Englewood, CO
Marilyn Sylvain, Bloomfield Hills, MI
Marc Talley, Bellevue, WA
Kathy Tamosaitis, Kennett Square, PA
Marion Taormina, Stuart, FL
Chris Taricani, Avon, CT
Kim Taylor, Englewood, CO
Catherine Tenbrook, Austin, TX
Caryn Thierbach, Cincinnati, OH

Marcella Thompson, Rockville, MD
Irene Thurman, Lynnwood, WA
Nancy Todaro, Las Vegas, NV
Linda Torres, Pleasant Hill, CA
Catherine Toscano, River Edge, NJ
Margaret Toth, Jenkintown, PA
Mary Townsend, San Antonio, TX
Kristen Trujillo, Rockville, MD
Joseph Tuccillo, Yardley, PA
Franklin Valentin, Mamaroneck, NY
Nancy Van Cleve, Jacksonville, FL
Luci Vathanadireg, Huntington Beach, CA
Cindy Vorauer, Strafford, PA
Lynne Wagner, Denver, CO
Bee Walcom, Las Vegas, NV
Kenny Walker, Denver, CO
Jeanette Wallace, Memphis, TN
Lisa Wallace, Bellevue, WA
Marjie Wallace, Bellevue, WA
Diana Walsh, Towson, MD
Kay Ward, Columbia, MD
Sue Ward, Dallas, TX
Alison Warner, Orange, CA
Sandra Wascher, San Diego, CA
Nancy Waterman, Hanover, MA
Sara Weertz, St. Clair Shores, MI
Mary Weinschreider, Birmingham, AL
Cheryl Wheeler, Kennett Square, PA
Bonnie White, Timonium, MD
Betty Wilbur, Wilmington, DE
Gilbert Wilbur, Wilmington, DE
Sam Wilson, Fairfax, VA
Marge Witten, Okemos, MI
Denise Wolford, Greenbrae, CA
Eileen Wozniak, Buffalo, NY
Doris Wrenn, Virginia Beach, VA
Sandy Wurth, Kansas City, KS
Mack Wylke, Richmond, VA

FABRIC NOTES

The photographs used on the cover and in chapter openings are from recent Calico Corners catalogs. Most of the furniture and fabrics featured are available through the Calico Corners stores across the country. For the store location nearest you, or for a current catalog, please call 1-800-213-6366.

Cover, Title Page, Desserts, Candy and Cookies

Upholstered furniture: Abbottswood, color Porcelain, cotton blue-and-white print

Pillows:
Hunt Club Washed, color Cobalt, solid blue twill
Bertie, color Blue, cotton check
Bertie, color Lime, cotton check
Bertie, color Yellow, cotton check

Table topper:
Chaucer, color Sunshine, small stripe

Brunch and Breads

Loveseat: Chucker, color Chambray, cotton lightweight denim

Tableskirt: Chucker, color Chambray, cotton lightweight denim, with band of Bombay, color Lake cotton plaid

Flanged Pillow: Sandy Hook, color Fiesta (yellow), cotton print check

Ruffled Pillow: Bombay, color Lake, cotton woven plaid

Chair: Lavait, color Sunblu, cotton floral print

Appetizers and Beverages

Sofa and draperies: Tiverton, color Amber, cotton floral print

Pillows, throw and ottoman top: Ansley, color Persimmon, rayon scroll jacquard

Soups and Salads

Pillow: Basketweave, color Periwinkle, cotton printed plaid

Table topper: Picnic, color Periwinkle, cotton print with fruit design

Tableskirt: Checkers, color Red, cotton print

Meat, Poultry and Seafood

Draperies/Loveseat: Brocade, color Rouge, cotton floral print on damask ground

Balloon Shade: Kirov, color Rose, silk check

Dining chairs: Ballet, color Aqua, cotton/rayon jacquard floral upholstery

Wing chairs: Chippendale, color Antique, cotton/rayon bargello tapestry

Screen/Runner: Porto, color Celedon, cotton/polyester damask

Vegetables and Side Dishes

Table topper: McCall, color Vintage, cotton woven stripe with band of Big Spring stripe, color Vintage

Pillows:
Home Sweet Home, color Multi, cotton birdhouse print
McCall, color Vintage, cotton woven stripe
Pistol River, color Natural/Denim, cotton woven stripe

Pasta

Table topper: LeMans, color Red small floral with wide banding of Mulhouse plaid, color Red; large floral undercloth of Lausanne, color Yellow

Napkins: Montauban allover leaf pattern, colors Yellow and Red

Cakes and Pies

Floral chair: Montclair, color Pink, cotton print on damask basecloth

Striped chair: Dylan, color Pink, stripe on damask basecloth

Draperies: Victoria Bay, color Rose, rayon moiré plaid

INDEX

Accompaniments. *See also*
    Sauces
    Aïoli, 116
    Berry Coulis, 10
    Bread-and-Butter Pickles, 117
    Cranberry Orange Relish, 117
    Crème Fraîche, 101
    Dijon Vinaigrette, 108
    Italian Salsa, 38
    Mustard Butter, 32
    Seafood Mayonnaise, 96
    Spiced Cranberries, 116
    Spinach Dressing, 33
    Strawberry Almond Sauce, 20
    Tomato Coulis, 19

Almonds
    Almond Toffee, 149
    Biscotti, 151
    Bok Choy Salad, 62
    Honey Cakes, 155
    Mandarin Tossed Salad, 66
    Strawberry Almond French
        Crepes, 20
    Strawberry Almond Sauce, 20

Appetizers
    Artichoke Cheese Squares, 31
    Black Bean Salsa, 38
    Bleu Cheese Flan, 43
    Caponata, 37
    Cowboy Caviar, 40
    Crab de Jonge, 32
    Dim Sum Dumplings, 33
    Ham Roll-Ups, 34
    Hot Artichoke Spread, 41
    Italian Salsa, 38
    Marinated Shrimp, 35
    Middle Eastern Eggplant
        Dip, 40
    Sausalito Crab Dip, 41
    Shrimp Pâté, 42
    Shrimp Strudel, 34
    Spiced-Up Pecans, 31
    Spinach and Cheese Squares, 35
    Tomato Bruschetta, 39
    Tuna Pâté, 42
    Vegetable Pizza, 36
    Zucchini Gorgonzola
        Rounds, 36

Apples
    Apple Currant Muffins, 26
    Apples in Baskets, 149
    Bread Pudding with
        Apples, 148
    Cranberry Apple Crisp, 143
    Mincemeat Pies, 178
    Stuffed Pork Loin, 81
    Swedish Apple Pie, 175

Apricots
    Sachertorte, 172
    Stuffed Pork Loin, 81
    Summer Cottage Breakfast
        Pudding, 14

Artichokes
    Artichoke Cheese
        Squares, 31
    Caesar Pasta Salad, 121
    Ham Roll-Ups, 34
    Hot Artichoke Spread, 41
    Peppercorn Pasta Sauce, 137
    Point Barrow Seafood
        Casserole, 97
    Rice Salad with Artichokes, 67
    Sausalito Crab Dip, 41

Asparagus
    Asparagus and Cashew
        Stir-Fry, 99
    Bow Tie Chicken and Vegetable
        Salad, 120
    The Ultimate Quiche, 16

Bananas
    Banana Cake, 163
    Banana Citrus Compote, 9

Beans
    Black Bean Salsa, 38
    Chalupas, 79
    Lamb Chops with Cannellini
        and Spinach, 78
    Monastery Lentil Soup, 50
    Red Beans and Rice, 100
    Tamale Pie, 77
    Tuscan-Style Beans, 100
    Vegetable Casserole, 112
    Vegetarian Chili, 110

Beef
    Barbecued Brisket, 69
    Beefy Egg Brunch, 11
    Damn Good Stew, 70
    Ground Beef Stroganoff, 75
    Italian Meat Loaf, 74
    Jamaican Stuffed Pumpkin, 72
    Pepper Steak, 71
    Sirloin Steaks with Bleu Cheese
        Butter, 73
    Skillet Dinner Mexicana, 76
    Spaghetti Pie, 127
    Spicy New England Pot
        Roast, 70
    Tamale Pie, 77

Berries. *See also* individual kinds
    Berry Cloud with Brandied
        Cream, 139
    Fall Mimosas, 9

Beverages
    Fall Mimosas, 9
    Fruit Shake, 45
    Holiday Eggnog, 44
    Melon Cooler, 45
    Yogi Tea, 44

Blueberries
    Blueberry Breakfast Cake, 24
    Blueberry Cheesecake, 140
    Blueberry Cream Salad, 58
    Blueberry Sauce, 140

Breads
    Apple Currant Muffins, 26
    Blueberry Breakfast Cake, 24
    Cream Cheese Coffee
        Cake, 25
    Fabulous French Toast, 22
    Famous Buttermilk Pancakes, 22
    Gingerbread, 144
    Gingerbread Waffles, 23
    Grandma's Cinnamon
        Rolls, 27
    Jalapeño Corn Bread, 29
    Lemon Bread, 28
    Oatmeal Muffins, 26
    Orange Poppy Seed Scones, 28
    Southern-Style Biscuits, 24

    Strawberry Bread, 29
    Texas Corn Bread, 15

Broccoli
    Broccoli and Cranberry
        Slaw, 62
    Broccoli and Fennel, 102
    Broccoli Egg Bake, 10
    Broccoli Supreme, 101
    Cheesy Chicken Casserole, 86
    Cream of Broccoli Soup, 47
    Sicilian Fusilli with Broccoli, 134

Bulgur
    Bulgur Pilaf, 115
    Vegetarian Chili, 110

Cabbage
    Bok Choy Salad, 62
    Broccoli and Cranberry
        Slaw, 62
    Napa Cabbage Slaw, 63
    Unstuffed Cabbage, 78

Cakes
    Banana Cake, 163
    Brown Sugar Pound Cake, 170
    Chocolate Fudge Cake, 164
    Chocolate Zucchini Cake, 165
    Hazelnut Cake, 167
    Japanese Fruit Cake, 166
    Lemon Pound Cake, 170
    Oatmeal Cake, 167
    Pear Cake, 169
    Pineapple Upside-Down
        Cake, 168
    Potato Cake, 168
    Rum Cake, 171
    Sachertorte, 172
    Sherry Cake, 173
    Walnut Pumpkin Roll, 174

Candy
    Almond Toffee, 149
    Foolproof Chocolate Fudge, 150
    Peanut Butter Balls, 150

Carrots
    Carrot and Ginger Soup, 48
    Carrot Soufflé, 102

Cashews
Asparagus and Cashew
    Stir-Fry, 99
Chicken with Cashews, 88
Pasta Salad del Sol, 124
Stuffed Pork Loin, 81

Cheese
Artichoke Cheese Squares, 31
Bleu Cheese Flan, 43
Blueberry Cheesecake, 140
Broccoli Egg Bake, 10
Cheesy Chicken Casserole, 86
Chèvre and Arugula Salad, 61
Chocolate Cheese Pie, 176
Cornmeal Dumplings, 76
Cream Cheese
    Frosting, 159, 165
Enchiladas Mañanitas, 90
German Chocolate
    Cheesecake, 141
Ham Roll-Ups, 34
Italian Meat Loaf, 74
Linguini with Salsa
    Cruda, 134
Mexican Corn Pudding, 104
Mexican Egg Puff, 12
Mexican Grits, 112
Point Barrow Seafood
    Casserole, 97
Pork Sausage and Cheese
    Manicotti, 128
Potato Pierogies, 105
Seafood Vera Cruz, 93
Shrimp Strudel, 34
Sicilian Fusilli with
    Broccoli, 134
Sirloin Steaks with Bleu
    Cheese Butter, 73
Southwestern Seafood
    Lasagna, 131
Spinach and Cheese
    Squares, 35
Sunday Brunch Strata, 13
Superb Cheese Soufflé, 17
Texas Corn Bread, 15
The Ultimate Quiche, 16
Tuna Pâté, 42
Zucchini Gorgonzola
    Rounds, 36

Cheesecakes
Blueberry Cheesecake, 140
German Chocolate
    Cheesecake, 141

Chicken
Barbecued Chicken, 84
Bow Tie Chicken and Vegetable
    Salad, 120
Buffet Chicken, 87
Cheesy Chicken Casserole, 86
Chicken and Zucchini
    Risotto, 84
Chicken Chili, 89
Chicken Curry, 91
Chicken with Cashews, 88
Chicken with Mushroom
    Sauce, 86
Cordon Bleu Soup, 51
Curried Chicken Salad, 60
Dim Sum Dumplings, 33
Enchiladas Mañanitas, 90
Lazy Chicken Dinner, 85
Lemon Chicken, 88
Ravioli and Chicken with
    Pesto Sauce, 128
Summer Chicken Salad, 59
Sweet-and-Sour Chicken, 92

Chocolate
Brownie Decadence, 152
Chocolate Angel Pie, 176
Chocolate Cheese Pie, 176
Chocolate Chip Cookies, 153
Chocolate Fudge Cake, 164
Chocolate Fudge Frosting, 164
Chocolate Glaze, 142
Chocolate Mousse Dessert, 142
Chocolate Strawberry
    Tart, 182
Chocolate Zucchini Cake, 165
Foolproof Chocolate
    Fudge, 150
German Chocolate
    Cheesecake, 141
Gooey Baked Alaska, 145
Grand Marnier Sauce, 145
Hazelnut Cake, 167
Mocha Frosting, 172
Peanut Butter Balls, 150

Peanut Butter Cookies, 157
Rocca, 160

Coconut
Coconut Frosting, 166
Coconut Pecan Topping, 141
German Chocolate
    Cheesecake, 141
Japanese Fruit Cake, 166
Lemon Coconut Cookies, 156
Oatmeal Cake, 167
Pineapple Drop Cookies, 158

Coffee
Chocolate Glaze, 142
Chocolate Mousse
    Dessert, 142
Gooey Baked Alaska, 145
Mocha Frosting, 172

Cookies
Bird's Nest Cookies, 151
Biscotti, 151
Brownie Decadence, 152
Cheesecake Bars, 153
Chocolate Chip Cookies, 153
Gooey Butter Squares, 154
Grandmother's Ginger
    Cookies, 154
Honey Cakes, 155
Lemon Coconut Cookies, 156
Lemon Supremes, 156
Peanut Butter Cookies, 157
Pecan Sandies, 158
Pineapple Drop Cookies, 158
Quick Pumpkin Bars, 159
Raspberry Bars, 160
Rocca, 160
Smashed Oatmeal Cookies, 157
Sour Cream Nut Horns, 161
Teatime Tassies, 161

Corn
Clam and Smoked Salmon
    Chowder, 48
Corn and Tomato Gratin, 103
Cowboy Caviar, 40
Jalapeño Corn Bread, 29
Mexican Corn Pudding, 104
Texas Corn Bread, 15

Crab Meat
Crab de Jonge, 32
Crab Imperial, 94
Crab Meat Pasta Parmesan, 129
Eastern Shore Crab Cakes, 94
Point Barrow Seafood
    Casserole, 97
Sausalito Crab Dip, 41
Southwestern Seafood
    Lasagna, 131
Steamboat Cream of Crab
    Soup, 50
Supper Salad Mold, 59

Cranberries
Broccoli and Cranberry
    Slaw, 62
Cranberry Apple Crisp, 143
Cranberry Orange Relish, 117
Roasted Honey Pepper
    Pork, 80
Sliced Oranges with Berry
    Coulis, 10
Spiced Cranberries, 116
Spicy New England Pot
    Roast, 70
Stuffed Pork Loin, 81

Crepes
Scrambled Egg Brunch
    Crepes, 21
Strawberry Almond French
    Crepes, 20

Cucumbers
Bread-and-Butter Pickles, 117
Chilled Shrimp and Cucumber
    Soup, 57
Cucumber Penne, 133

Decorating
Accents, 15, 51, 89, 97, 125
Armcovers, 119
Bath, 155
Bed Coverings, 11, 25, 55, 63
Color, 43, 51, 137
Fabric Care, 77
Files, 183
Flowers, 17
Furniture, 21, 85, 139, 171

Furniture Arrangement, 65
Mixing Fabrics, 81, 113, 135, 159, 175, 179
Napkins, 79, 121
Patio Cushions, 127, 133
Pillows, 39, 45
Seasonal, 11, 25, 37, 39, 45, 47, 65, 87, 103, 111
Slipcovers, 47, 87, 163, 181
Storage, 27
Table Coverings, 57, 61, 69, 73, 83, 95, 99, 103, 107, 127
Throws, 37
Wall Hangings, 13, 91
Window Treatments, 25, 71, 75, 173, 177, 179

Desserts. *See also* Cakes; Candy; Cookies; Pies; Tarts
Apples in Baskets, 149
Berry Cloud with Brandied Cream, 139
Blueberry Cheesecake, 140
Bread Pudding with Apples, 148
Chocolate Mousse Dessert, 142
Cranberry Apple Crisp, 143
Flan, 143
German Chocolate Cheesecake, 141
Gingerbread, 144
Gooey Baked Alaska, 145
Ice Cream with Grand Marnier Sauce, 145
Lemon Soufflé with Strawberry Sauce, 146
Linzertorte, 147
Peach Cobbler, 147
Plum Kuchen, 148

Dumplings
Cornmeal Dumplings, 76
Dim Sum Dumplings, 33

Eggplant
Caponata, 37
Middle Eastern Eggplant Dip, 40
Pepper Ratatouille, 106
Ratatouille, 107

Eggs
Beefy Egg Brunch, 11
Broccoli Egg Bake, 10
Fabulous French Toast, 22
Flan, 143
Holiday Eggnog, 44
Mexican Egg Puff, 12
Mushroom Spinach Strata, 12
Scrambled Egg Brunch Crepes, 21
Soufflé Roll with Spinach Filling and Tomato Coulis, 18
Spinach Quiche, 16
Summer Cottage Breakfast Pudding, 14
Sunday Brunch Strata, 13
Superb Cheese Soufflé, 17
The Ultimate Quiche, 16

Frostings. *See also* Glazes; Toppings
Caramel Frosting, 169
Chocolate Fudge Frosting, 164
Coconut Frosting, 166
Cream Cheese Frosting, 159, 165
Mocha Frosting, 172

Fruit. *See also* individual kinds
Cream of Cantaloupe Soup, 56
Fall Mimosas, 9
Fruit Shake, 45
Melon Cooler, 45
Peach Cobbler, 147

Glazes
Chocolate Glaze, 142
Sherry Glaze, 173

Ham
Broccoli Egg Bake, 10
Cordon Bleu Soup, 51
Ham Roll-Ups, 34
Jamaican Stuffed Pumpkin, 72
Pasta Salad del Sol, 124
Pumpkin and Prosciutto Lasagna, 126
Tuscan-Style Beans, 100

Hazelnuts
Berry Cloud with Brandied Cream, 139
Hazelnut Cake, 167
Linzertorte, 147

Ice Cream
Gooey Baked Alaska, 145
Ice Cream with Grand Marnier Sauce, 145

Lamb
Lamb Chops with Cannellini and Spinach, 78
Unstuffed Cabbage, 78

Lemon
Citrus Sauce, 144
Ice Cream with Grand Marnier Sauce, 145
Lemon Bread, 28
Lemon Chicken, 88
Lemon Coconut Cookies, 156
Lemon Crunch Pie, 177
Lemon Pound Cake, 170
Lemon Rice, 114
Lemon Sauce, 23
Lemon Soufflé with Strawberry Sauce, 146
Lemon Supremes, 156

Mushrooms
Blackened Shrimp with Pasta, 130
Ground Beef Stroganoff, 75
Mushrooms Berkeley, 104
Mushroom Spinach Strata, 12

Nuts. *See also* individual kinds
Banana Cake, 163
Linguini with Pistachios, 132
Pineapple Drop Cookies, 158
Raspberry Bars, 160
Rocca, 160

Orange
Citrus Sauce, 144
Cranberry Orange Relish, 117
Grand Marnier Sauce, 145

Mandarin Tossed Salad, 66
Orange Basil Dressing, 124
Orange Poppy Seed Scones, 28
Pasta Salad del Sol, 124
Pretzel Salad, 58
Sliced Oranges with Berry Coulis, 10
Super Spinach Salad, 64

Pasta
Beer-Spiked Shrimp and Spaghetti, 130
Blackened Shrimp with Pasta, 130
Bow Tie Chicken and Vegetable Salad, 120
Caesar Pasta Salad, 121
Crab Meat Pasta Parmesan, 129
Cucumber Penne, 133
Greek Tortellini Salad, 122
Ground Beef Stroganoff, 75
Linguini with Pistachios, 132
Linguini with Salsa Cruda, 134
Linguini with Tuna Caper Sauce, 129
Mediterranean Salad with Basil, 123
Mexican Bow Ties, 119
Pasta Salad del Sol, 124
Pasta with Roasted Peppers, 136
Penne with Tomato Vodka Sauce, 135
Peppercorn Pasta Sauce, 137
Pork Sausage and Cheese Manicotti, 128
Pumpkin and Prosciutto Lasagna, 126
Ravioli and Chicken with Pesto Sauce, 128
Shrimp and Pasta Provençal, 132
Sicilian Fusilli with Broccoli, 134
Southwestern Seafood Lasagna, 131
Spaghetti Pie, 127
Stuffed Zucchini, 111
Tortellini Antipasto Salad, 125
Tuscan Pasta, 136

Pastry
Apples in Baskets, 149
Pie Pastry, 180

Peanut Butter
Peanut Butter Balls, 150
Peanut Butter Cookies, 157

Pears
Pear Cake, 169
Pear Tart, 181

Peas
Bow Tie Chicken and Vegetable
    Salad, 120
Cowboy Caviar, 40
Summer Chicken Salad, 59
Veal Spiedini, 82
Vegetable Casserole, 112

Pecans
Brownie Decadence, 152
Cheesecake Bars, 153
Chocolate Angel Pie, 176
Coconut Pecan Topping, 141
Foolproof Chocolate Fudge, 150
German Chocolate
    Cheesecake, 141
Gooey Butter Squares, 154
Japanese Fruit Cake, 166
Minted Wild Rice, 114
Peanut Butter Cookies, 157
Pecan Caramel Tart, 183
Pecan Praline Topping, 152
Pecan Sandies, 158
Potato Cake, 168
Spiced-Up Pecans, 31
Teatime Tassies, 151
Wild Rice with Pecans, 115
World Class Pumpkin Pie, 180

Peppers
Black Bean Salsa, 38
Bread and Butter Pickles, 117
Chalupas, 79
Chicken Chili, 89
Greek Tortellini Salad, 122
Jalapeño Corn Bread, 29
Mexican Bow Ties, 119
Mushrooms Berkeley, 104

Pasta with Roasted
    Peppers, 136
Pepper Ratatouille, 106
Pepper Steak, 71
Ratatouille, 107
Skillet Dinner Mexicana, 76
Vegetable Casserole, 112
Yellow Pepper Soup, 52

Pies. *See also* Tarts
Chocolate Angel Pie, 176
Chocolate Cheese Pie, 176
Green Tomato Pie, 178
Lemon Crunch Pie, 177
Mincemeat Pies, 178
Pie Pastry, 180
Purple Plum Pie, 179
Swedish Apple Pie, 175
World Class Pumpkin Pie, 180

Pineapple
Pasta Salad del Sol, 124
Pineapple Drop Cookies, 158
Pineapple Upside-Down
    Cake, 168
Pretzel Salad, 58
Sweet-and-Sour Chicken, 92

Pine Nuts
Bulgur Pilaf, 115
Sicilian Fusilli with Broccoli, 134
Veal Spiedini, 82

Plum
Plum Kuchen, 148
Purple Plum Pie, 179

Pork. *See also* Sausage
Barbecued Ribs, 80
Chalupas, 79
Roasted Honey Pepper Pork, 80
Stuffed Pork Loin, 81

Potatoes
German Potato Salad, 65
Grilled Potato and Onion
    Packets, 106
Italian Potato Soup, 52
Potato Cake, 168
Potato Pierogies, 105

Prunes
Buffet Chicken, 87
Stuffed Pork Loin, 81

Pumpkin
Jamaican Stuffed Pumpkin, 72
Pumpkin and Prosciutto
    Lasagna, 126
Quick Pumpkin Bars, 159
Walnut Pumpkin Roll, 174
World Class Pumpkin
    Pie, 180

Quiches
Spinach Quiche, 16
The Ultimate Quiche, 16

Raspberries
Linzertorte, 147
Raspberry Bars, 160
Sliced Oranges with Berry
    Coulis, 10

Rice
Champagne Rice Pilaf, 113
Chicken and Zucchini
    Risotto, 84
Chicken with Mushroom
    Sauce, 86
Curried Chicken Salad, 60
Jambalaya, 82
Lemon Rice, 114
Minted Wild Rice, 114
Picnic Rice Salad, 67
Red Beans and Rice, 100
Rice Salad with
    Artichokes, 67
Summer Chicken Salad, 59
Unstuffed Cabbage, 78
Wild Rice with Pecans, 115

Salad Dressings
Basil Viniagrette, 123
Dijon Vinaigrette, 108
Hoisin Dressing, 120
Mint Vinaigrette, 122
Napa Dressing, 63
Orange Basil Dressing, 124
Spicy Vinaigrette, 66
Trastevere Dressing, 61

Salads
Blueberry Cream Salad, 58
Bok Choy Salad, 62
Bow Tie Chicken and Vegetable
    Salad, 120
Broccoli and Cranberry Slaw, 62
Caesar Pasta Salad, 121
Chèvre and Arugula Salad, 61
Curried Chicken Salad, 60
German Potato Salad, 65
Greek Tortellini Salad, 122
Mandarin Tossed Salad, 66
Mediterranean Salad with
    Basil, 123
Mexican Bow Ties, 119
Napa Cabbage Slaw, 63
Napa Dressing, 63
Pacific Rim Caesar Salad, 64
Pasta Salad del Sol, 124
Picnic Rice Salad, 67
Pretzel Salad, 58
Rice Salad with
    Artichokes, 67
Summer Chicken Salad, 59
Super Spinach Salad, 64
Supper Salad Mold, 59
Tortellini Antipasto Salad, 125

Salmon
Clam and Smoked Salmon
    Chowder, 48
Grilled Salmon with
    Shrimp, 93

Sauces
Béchamel Sauce, 126
Blueberry Sauce, 140
Citrus Sauce, 144
Enchilada Sauce, 90
Grand Marnier Sauce, 145
Lemon Sauce, 23
Peppercorn Pasta Sauce, 137
Strawberry Almond Sauce, 20
Strawberry Sauce, 146

Sausage
Caesar Pasta Salad, 121
Italian Meat Loaf, 74
Italian Potato Soup, 52
Jambalaya, 82

Pork Sausage and Cheese
Manicotti, 128
Sunday Brunch Strata, 13
Texas Corn Bread, 15
Tortellini Antipasto Salad, 125

Seafood. *See also* individual kinds
Cioppino, 49
Clam and Smoked Salmon
Chowder, 48
Crawfish Étouffée, 95
Seafood Vera Cruz, 93

Shrimp
Beer-Spiked Shrimp and
Spaghetti, 130
Blackened Shrimp with
Pasta, 130
Caesar Pasta Salad, 121
Chilled Shrimp and Cucumber
Soup, 57
Cioppino, 49
Grilled Salmon with Shrimp, 93
Marinated Shrimp, 35
Point Barrow Seafood
Casserole, 97
Shrimp and Pasta
Provençal, 132
Shrimp Pâté, 42
Shrimp Strudel, 34
Southwestern Seafood
Lasagna, 131

Side Dishes. *See also* Rice
Bread-and-Butter Pickles, 117
Bulgur Pilaf, 115
Cornmeal Dumplings, 76
Cranberry Orange Relish, 117
Mexican Grits, 112
Spiced Cranberries, 116

Soufflés
Carrot Soufflé, 102
Lemon Soufflé with Strawberry
Sauce, 146

Soufflé Roll with Spinach Filling
and Tomato Coulis, 18
Superb Cheese Soufflé, 17

Soups
Carrot and Ginger Soup, 48
Chilled Shrimp and Cucumber
Soup, 57
Cioppino, 49
Clam and Smoked Salmon
Chowder, 48
Cordon Bleu Soup, 51
Cream of Broccoli Soup, 47
Cream of Cantaloupe Soup, 56
Gazpacho, 56
Italian Potato Soup, 52
Monastery Lentil Soup, 50
Ribollita, 53
Steamboat Cream of Crab
Soup, 50
Tomato and Leek Bisque, 55
Tuscan Tomato Bread Soup, 54
Yellow Pepper Soup, 52

Spinach
Lamb Chops with Cannellini
and Spinach, 78
Mushroom Spinach Strata, 12
Soufflé Roll with Spinach Filling
and Tomato Coulis, 18
Spinach and Cheese
Squares, 19
Spinach Dressing, 33
Spinach Quiche, 16
Super Spinach Salad, 64

Strawberries
Chocolate Strawberry Tart, 182
Lemon Soufflé with Strawberry
Sauce, 146
Strawberry Almond French
Crepes, 20
Strawberry Almond Sauce, 20
Strawberry Bread, 29
Strawberry Sauce, 146

Sweet Potatoes
Rum-Spiced Yams, 109
Sweet Potato Casserole, 109

Tarts
Chocolate Strawberry
Tart, 182
Pear Tart, 181
Pecan Caramel Tart, 183

Tomatoes
Chicken Chili, 89
Corn and Tomato Gratin, 103
Enchilada Sauce, 90
Gazpacho, 56
Green Tomato Pie, 178
Italian Salsa, 38
Linguini with Salsa Cruda, 134
Mexican Bow Ties, 119
Penne with Tomato Vodka
Sauce, 135
Peppercorn Pasta Sauce, 137
Ratatouille, 107
Roasted Tomato and Basil
Casserole, 108
Soufflé Roll with Spinach
Filling and Tomato
Coulis, 18
Tomato and Leek Bisque, 55
Tomato Bruschetta, 39
Tomato Coulis, 19
Trastevere Dressing, 61
Tuscan Tomato Bread
Soup, 54

Toppings
Coconut Pecan Topping, 141
Pecan Praline Topping, 152

Tuna
Linguini with Tuna Caper
Sauce, 129
Mediterranean Salad with
Basil, 123
Seafood Mayonnaise, 96

Tuna Pâté, 42
Tuna Steaks with Seafood
Mayonnaise, 96

Veal
Veal Ragout, 83
Veal Spiedini, 82

Vegetables. *See also* individual
kinds; Salads; Soups
Broccoli and Fennel, 102
Damn Good Stew, 70
Lazy Chicken Dinner, 85
Pepper Ratatouille, 106
Pepper Steak, 71
Spicy New England Pot
Roast, 70
Sweet-and-Sour Chicken, 92
Vegetable Pizza, 36
Vegetarian Chili, 110

Walnuts
Bird's Nest Cookies, 151
Broccoli and Cranberry
Slaw, 62
Brown Sugar Pound Cake, 170
Oatmeal Cake, 167
Sachertorte, 172
Sirloin Steaks with Bleu Cheese
Butter, 73
Smashed Oatmeal Cookies, 157
Sour Cream Nut Horns, 161
Swedish Apple Pie, 175
Walnut Pumpkin Roll, 174

Zucchini
Chicken and Zucchini
Risotto, 84
Chocolate Zucchini Cake, 165
Ratatouille, 107
Ravioli and Chicken with Pesto
Sauce, 128
Stuffed Zucchini, 111
Zucchini Gorgonzola
Rounds, 36

ORDER INFORMATION

For additional copies of

CALICO **Cooks!**

send:

$15.00 plus $3.50 postage and handling for each book

to:

Calico Corners
203 Gale Lane
Kennett Square, Pennsylvania 19348

or:

Call 1-800-213-6366 to order a cookbook, to request a current catalog, or for the store location near you.

VISA, MasterCard, and Discover accepted.

Make checks payable to Calico Corners.

Please add sales tax if shipping to the following states:

Alabama	Kansas	Ohio
Arizona	Louisiana	Oklahoma
California	Maryland	Pennsylvania
Colorado	Massachusetts	Tennessee
Connecticut	Michigan	Texas
District of	Minnesota	Utah
Columbia	Missouri	Virginia
Florida	Nevada	Washington
Georgia	New Jersey	Wisconsin
Illinois	New York	
Indiana	North Carolina	